"There is no passion to be found playing small – in settling for a life that is less than the one you are capable of living."

Nelson Mandela[1]

"Have a clear plan or strategy to translate your success philosophy into desired results. Adopt an effective work ethic, with a laser-focus and requisite execution strategies to produce results."

Archibald Marwizi[2]

Copyright

Life Planning Handbook: A life plan is the key to personal growth, by J. S. Wellman, published by Extra-mile Publishing, Box 465, Thompsons Station, TN 37179, copyright 2021, J. S. Wellman

ISBN   978-1-952359-32-3   (paperback)
ISBN   978-1-952359-33-0   (ebook)

For more information
about the Life Planning Series:

www.lifeplanningtools.com

Life Planning Handbook

A life plan is the key to personal growth.

LIFE PLANNING SERIES
J.S. WELLMAN

J. S. Wellman

Extra-mile Publishing

Free PDF

Wise
Decision-Making

[Get the ebook version for 99 cents]

We want to give you a <u>free</u> copy of:

Wise Decision-Making:
You can make good choices.

This book will help you make good decisions
in your life, career, family . . .

Free PDF:
www.lifeplanningtools.link/howtodecide

eBook for 99 cents:
https://www.amazon.com/dp/B09SYGWRVL

Ebook

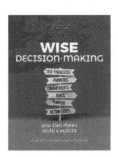

Free PDF

Life Planning Series

The Primary Life Principles

**These books will help you live a better lifestyle,
be content, and have a successful life.**

CHOOSE INTEGRITY	**Life Principle:** Be honest, live with integrity, and base your life on truth.
CHOOSE FRIENDS WISELY	**Life Principle:** Choose your friends wisely.
CHOOSE THE RIGHT WORDS	**Life Principle:** Guard your speech.
CHOOSE GOOD WORK HABITS	**Life Principle:** Be diligent and a hard worker.
CHOOSE FINANCIAL RESPONSIBILITY	**Life Principle:** Do not love money or worship wealth.
SCAN ME	**Scan the Q/R code to the left with your phone to check on availability of all books in the Life Planning Series. These five will be published in 2022.**

TABLE OF CONTENTS

Personal Message From the Author

The general purpose of this book and the Life Planning Series is to encourage you to pursue actions and character traits that will produce a better life. The book series will address 15 to 25 significant activities or traits that help people improve their lives and live their best life. The Planning Handbook's focus is on producing a Life Plan for your total life.

Understand that you can improve or acquire high personal character and outstanding habits, no matter how good or bad your life may be at this moment. High personal character and good life habits can be achieved and they will allow you to live a better life.

Know that you don't have to read all the books in the Life Planning Series to make a significant change or improvement in your life.

This is a progressive journey. Achieve your objectives one step at a time. You may just want to learn more about the basic principles of living a better life. This Series and the Handbook will provide you with a foundation for decisions that relate to your lifestyle, goals, priorities, and commitments.

The key to developing high character and making good decisions in your life is *intentionality*. This Handbook and the Life Planning Series will help you identify the path you want to travel, but you will have to be intentional about walking that path if you want to make progress toward the goal of living a better life.

Know that change will require making good decisions, establishing important core values, setting priorities, and making commitments. This book will help you identify the values in your life that will produce high personal character and good habits.

Remember, all actions (both words and deeds) have consequences. These consequences will impact you and all those around you.

Lastly, the very simple formula for success is: "*Decide you want to do it and work at it regularly*."

This book will give you guidance and we will even provide coaching if you want it. If you want to improve your life, just commit and carry through. We are here to help!

Decide to be the very best you can be!

Life Planning Series

Before reading this Handbook it will be useful if you know about our Life Planning Series. This series examines major personal characteristics, traits, and habits that are fundamental influencers in your life. Each book will include a Life Analysis focused on the subject of the book and then help you develop a plan to improve *that particular area* in your life. In addition, we can provide coaching assistance for those who want hands-on help.

Following is an outline of the Life Planning Series. See the "Next Steps" section at the end of this book for more details on our books and coaching assistance.

Life Planning Series

It is our objective in these books to help you choose the best path and give you tools to make good decisions in your life journey.

All the books will be meaningful to a general reading audience, but because the Christian viewpoint brings a different approach to many of these subjects and concepts, that perspective will be addressed in a separate Christian Wisdom Series.

The initial plan is to publish books on the following topics:

Subjects		Life Principle
Personal Character:		
Integrity*	honesty, truth, compromise/standing firm, justice, fairness	Be honest, live with integrity, and base Life on truth.
Reputation	respect, responsibility, sincerity	Earn the respect of others.
Leadership	power, decisiveness, courage, influence, loyalty	Lead well and be a loyal follower.
Identity/Self-Image	humor, being genuine, authenticity, confidence	Be confident in who you are.
Wisdom	discernment, correction, folly, foolishness	Seek knowledge, understanding, and wisdom.

Personal Relationships:

Friends*	Friends, associates, acquaintances	Choose your friends wisely.
Family	Honor, parenting, discipline	Honor your family.
Love	Love is . . .	Love one another.
Compassion	humility, mercy, goodness, kindness	Treat others as you want to be treated.
Forgiveness	reject grudges and revenge	Forgive others; do not hold grudges or take revenge.

Self-Control:

Speech*		Guard your speech.
Anger	self-control, self-discipline, patience	Always be under control.
Addiction	moderation, life balance	Live a life of balance and moderation, not excess.
Immorality	temptation	Set high moral standards.

Work Ethic:

Diligence*	perseverance, resilience, energy, apathy, laziness	Be diligent and a hard worker.
Trustworthiness	dependability, reliability, responsibility	Be trustworthy, dependable, and reliable.
Skills	curiosity, knowledge, education, abilities	Seek excellence; strive to do everything well.

Wealth:

Money*	wealth, poverty	Make sound financial choices.
Gratitude	generosity, thankfulness, gratefulness	Be thankful, grateful, and generous.

*The first subject listed under each of the categories above make up the Primary Life Principles.

After the initial launch in the first quarter of 2022 the books will be published in 4 to 8 week intervals. Choose the subjects and products that work for you and your needs.

LIFE PLANNING SERIES
J.S. WELLMAN

PRELUDE

Character is like a tree and reputation like its shadow.
The shadow is what we think of it;
the tree is the real thing.
Abraham Lincoln[3]

The purpose of this Handbook is to assist you in developing a life plan focused on your total life. Specifically we will investigate nine major categories of life experience to help you develop a plan that will assist you in implementing change in your life.

An African proverb says, *"Don't spend all day rejoicing on your bench. When you pray, move your feet!"* The message of this proverb is that if you want to accomplish something, it will not happen if you're sitting on your bench all day. Growth and improvement, including living a better life, require action and intentionality.

The good news is that you can use the information in this book to acquire knowledge that will help you follow a path to a better life. To do that you must follow Mr. Lincoln's advice in his quote at the top of the page. Examine the real you not at the cloud or shadow you may cast on the space around you.

The way to do that is:

- have a clear life strategy,
- adopt an effective work ethic, and
- develop action plans to achieve the desired results.

Intentionality with a plan is the
foundation for making progress!

Introduction

*"If you want a happy life, tie it to a goal,
not to people or things."*
Albert Einstein[4]

General

Why should you spend valuable time developing a plan for your life? We believe that the answer to that question ultimately comes down to the desire to live a better life. Wise and successful people are very careful how they live, and their intent is to make the most of every opportunity. If you simply let life happen and take little interest in where your life is heading, the world around you can implode and you may not be able to recover easily.

A Life Plan will help you be ready for the difficulties as well as celebrate the successes. Having a plan, and particularly working through the process of developing that plan, will help you live wisely, make good choices, and achieve a better life.

If you scanned the quote above like I did, you may have quickly agreed with the message that goals are very important. After I had entered the quote in the initial draft of this book, I realized I did not really agree with Einstein. I believe Albert got only part of it right, because caring and loving people can make life very pleasant, even joyful. Einstein was trying to make the point that goals in life are very important, and he was right. I suspect that Albert may have been a bit of a loner and, therefore, people were less important to him than goals.

I also suspect that Einstein was suggesting that people will disappoint us; they can change and become irritating. Goals will not be testy, change their minds, or question our motives; therefore, it is better to rely on a goal than a person to produce a happy life. Albert was married twice, and not surprisingly, neither marriage worked out.

Why Plan?

Some years ago our family (mom, dad, and three kids) took a month-long vacation trip. This was more than just a trip: this was *The* Family Trip West! Although our destination was California, reaching California was not really our goal, nor was it our purpose. We actually had several purposes, although we didn't state them formally at the time.

We had some emotional purposes: family fun and bonding, making memories. We had patriotic purposes: giving our kids a sense of their great country. We had educational purposes: learning about places we'd never seen before, and having new experiences. We wanted our small-Midwestern-town kids to get a real understanding of the physical beauty of our country: mountains, caves, oceans, deserts, rivers, cities. We wanted them to see the places they studied in their history and geography books. You get the idea!

In order to make this trip work, we planned for months. We joined Triple A. We read guidebooks, and checked out books from the library. The kids told us what they wanted to see and visit. We studied maps, plotted routes, and identified attractions. We asked friends what they enjoyed on similar trips. Of course, we left some room for flexibility, for changes of plans. We allowed for unexpected side trips, interesting things that might pop up along the way. But the general plan was established and in place before we left our driveway. As you have probably figured out, this was before the Internet.

Because we had planned carefully, we didn't miss things. We knew which states we wanted to travel through. We knew what interesting things we wanted to see. We knew where those things were, and we planned our time and routes so that we wouldn't get back home and hear someone say, "Oh, you should have been at Carlsbad Caverns in the late afternoon rather than morning – the bats are fascinating, and you missed them!" Therefore, when we left home very early one June morning, we knew where we were headed, how we would get there, what sorts of things we'd do on the way – and we all had a sense of embarking on a great and exciting adventure.

That trip is a metaphor for what we want to do in this book. It would have been foolish for our family to hop in a van on a sunny June morning and "hope" we'd find California.

> "Hope" we'd see lots of good places on the way.
> "Hope" that at bedtime we'd be in towns rather than in a desert.
> "Hope" we'd find roads to get there and back.
> "Hope" we'd have the kind of clothes needed to be comfortable.
> "Hope" that Sea World would be open on the day we got there.

It would have been foolish to leave home without maps, without guidebooks – without plans. Yet, that's what many of us do in life. We may have some general goals (I'd like a family. I'd like a good job. I'd like to travel). But the reality is we are hoping or assuming those things will happen. Our vague goals can prompt actions (if I want a good job, I need an education) but even these things often happen more by chance than because we took deliberate action to ensure they would occur.

Our journey on this earth has a physical limit. In the physical sense, life has only one final destination. But life's journey itself has infinite possibilities. Planning that journey means that we won't get to the end of it and have the feeling, "I wish I'd done more of this. I never intended to be like that. I wasted years doing the other. I could have. I should have. I might have. If only . . ."

Admittedly, life throws us curves. Unexpected things happen – both flat tires and rainbows – for which we could never plan. But a plan can help us see beyond the unexpected. We can be ready to take advantage of the opportunities and to get through the challenges that life presents.

We may wish we'd known how to plan when we were young. But if we are now nearing retirement, is there any value to developing a Life Plan at our age? We firmly believe so! Planning can be beneficial regardless of your age or circumstances. It's never too late to look at what you are doing and where you are headed. You may be somewhere in Texas or Arizona in your metaphoric journey, but you haven't reached the West Coast yet! There are a lot of things between here and there that you can do, can achieve, can accomplish, can enjoy. So make plans to experience all the important things along the way!

Commitment

On February 19, 1519, the Spanish explorer Hernan Cortez set sail for Mexico. He had 11 ships, 110 sailors, and 533 soldiers. Previous explorers had failed to occupy the land, which had a population of 5 million people. Cortez ultimately conquered most of central and south America. He landed in Mexico and then ordered his men to *"Burn the ships!"*

Can you imagine yourself being a sailor or soldier and the crazy commander orders the ships to be burned? What would you have thought? What are the implications of this command? I can think of several important results:

- Retreat was not an option.

- They could not go home. There was no turning back.

- It was sink or swim; they were committed whether they liked it or not.

- They must stick with Plan A. Other plans were no longer possible.

Why do we mention this story in a life planning book? Just like Cortez, you should be serious about achieving your goals. Cortez's trip on the high seas was over. It was time to start anew. There was a definite period at the end of the sentence: it was time to move on.

You can relate this story to relationships or addictions. The old ways are gone and it's time to start a new chapter in your life. Thus, the focus of your planning process should be on new beginnings. It's time to focus on the present and the future and leave the past behind. In other words, *"Burn the ships!"*

This was a defining moment for the sailors because it eliminated the possibility of sailing back to the old world. They could not go back to life as usual. They could not decide to try this another time. The time was now. It eliminated the possibility of moving back into the past. It changed how they thought about their circumstances and the future.

They were not going home if this adventure did not work, so they had to make it work. Think of this planning process from that perspective.

It would be like taking a full-page ad in a local newspaper and announcing all your life goals, with a promise to report progress in the paper for the next 48 months. You have gone on record and it will be difficult to quietly back out because everybody knows. You will have to be serious about living a better life.

Encouragement

If you have a desire to make any significant changes in your life, then your next step should be to develop a Life Plan. It will give you a good perspective on life and provide a road map for the future. This book is written as a workbook or handbook. It is a hands-on "how to" book. Its purpose is to assist you in developing a total Life Plan. It is aimed at anyone 16 years or older. It will take you through the practical step-by-step process of developing life values, priorities, commitments, goals, and finally action steps to achieve those goals.

Although it is extensive, it's simple, so anyone can do it. The focus will be on the process of producing the plan, and very little time in convincing you to do it – we assume that's why you purchased the book.

This process would be the logical next step for anyone who has read a book in the Life Planning Series, but it stands on its own. It is not dependent on anything done in any of our Life Planning books. There are some similar sections and you may find it helpful to have those books available as you complete this planning process, but the process in this book is independent of the Life Planning Series.

Each book in the Life Planning Series addresses only one particular character trait or activity. In this Handbook, we will look at your entire life. If you want to dig a little deeper into a few particular traits, you should acquire the appropriate Life Planning Series book. Details of this series are provided at the end of this book.

Change

"Yesterday I was clever, so I wanted to change the world.
Today I am wise, so I am changing myself."
Patrick Ness[5]

This quote is a great advertisement for the personal growth industry. Another way this truth might be stated is, "*Get your own house in order before you attempt to redecorate for someone else.*" Another truth in this quote is the recognition that it is necessary to change or work on personal attributes or skills. No one in this life is perfect, although some people are in better shape than others because of circumstances totally outside their control.

Focus on just the last sentence of this quote for a moment. Now that I have become wise, I understand that I can change myself for the better. Wisdom has triggered change. For example, if you now understand the power of your words, you may decide to control your speech. Now that you understand the impact and influence of the friends in your life, you may decide that you need to select your friends more carefully. You may never have understood the importance of honesty and integrity. You may have grown up in an environment where truth and honesty were not modeled. However, life has now taught you the problems and difficulties that being untrustworthy can create.

Change can be frightening to many people. Most of us get very comfortable with the status quo and when change creeps up on us, or is thrust upon us like the COVID 19 pandemic, we often react badly. We fight change, we ignore change, and we reject the products of change. Then, at some point, we have to accept that our lives, our jobs, our families, or our health have changed.

The concepts and the commitments in this book are inherently about change. If you adopt a Life Principle, Life Priority, or a new Life Commitment, you are fostering change in your life. That may be alarming or exciting depending on your circumstances. We hope that it results in living a better life!

The subject of change could take up all the pages in this book. We could analyze all the professional books on this subject and lay out all the positive reasons and ways you could deal with change. We won't do that although we know that the fear of change may prevent you from using the wisdom in this book to improve your life.

Life is a series of decisions and changes. The many choices you make in life often produce change. Most of the changes that occur in our lives we accept and integrate quickly without a moment's thought. But the bigger changes, like trying to improve one's life, can have greater impact. To some, such change is a challenge, and they look forward to it. For others it can be a paralyzing thought that prevents anything from happening. Most of us fall in the middle of that spectrum.

An important characteristic here is that you are the one fostering the change. It is not being thrust upon you from some outside source. Thus, you ultimately have the ability to control the nature of that change. Our suggestion on the subject of controlling the improvement in your life is to let it happen. Don't try to change reality or the natural result of making wise decisions.

But that advice alone will not necessarily impact how you react to change. We will provide one current example of change that we hope will convince you not to resist change in your life, then, we will not return to this subject again.

Did you notice who survived the COVID-19 pandemic well? Massive changes in our economy and social relationships were thrust upon us overnight. People, businesses, and governments struggled to know what to do. Some did not fare well!

Just look around at the local businesses in your community. Who survived? Who did not? I can almost guarantee you that those who survived are the ones who embraced change. For example, the restaurants in my community reacted in three basic ways:

- They tried to maintain business as usual and fought all the regulations and rules.

- They reluctantly made changes in accordance with the local health or governmental guidelines.

- They fundamentally changed or expanded the core nature of their business and they thrived.

The key to the successful businesses was that they embraced the change. They may not have liked it but they recognized that their business was in the midst of fundamental change and they aggressively reacted to the nature of that change. Some of the restaurants closed their dining rooms completely and converted to carry-out only. Others used new ways and new locations to seat diners. Those businesses that accepted the challenge of change and responded aggressively and creatively fared much better than the others.

This was also evident in the sports world where the NBA, for example, created a bubble environment for their playoffs. All the games were played in one location, while the players were required to live in a quarantined environment.

What we want you to recognize is that those who managed change successfully, responded aggressively, and kept their eyes on the target were much more likely to succeed. Those who resisted change often buried their heads in the sand, or minimally and reluctantly complied with the new environment. They generally struggled and often failed.

Lastly, we offer this quote from Thomas Edison about perseverance, *"Many of life's failures are people who did not realize how close they were to success when they gave up."*[6] Giving up before you have finished or achieved your goal can be very tempting. Maybe you are just plain tired and you don't want to think about changing your life anymore. You may be frustrated because results have not been that positive. If you feel this way, we have three suggestions:

1. Talk to someone you trust.

2. Review your plans and activities. Maybe something needs to be changed or tweaked.

3. Take a break. Clear your head.

Typical Questions We Will Consider in This Planning Process

1. What do you want or need out of life?

2. How and where are you most effective?
    a. What are your gifts, talents, skills, and abilities?
    b. Are you using your skills and abilities wisely?

3. What are your priorities in life?
    a. How much time are you spending on priorities?
    b. How do your priorities line up with what you want to accomplish?

4. What do you want to accomplish before you die?
    a. Have you started?
    b. Are you having any success?
    c. Do you need to change direction?

5. What are your goals and objectives?
    a. Can you put them in writing?
    b. On what are they based?
    c. How will you accomplish them?

"Remember your dreams and fight for them. You must know what you want from life. There is just one thing that makes your dream become impossible: the fear of failure."
Paul Coelho[7]

SPECIAL NOTICE

To: the Christian reader
If you are a Christian, we strongly recommend reading Appendix A before you continue. It will change how you proceed through this book and how you develop your Life Plan.

Chapter 1

What is a Life Plan?

A Life Plan includes your life mission statement, your life goals,
and the actions and plans to achieve your life mission.
It is aimed at improving your future well-being.

GENERAL

Large corporations routinely spend millions preparing both short-term and long-term corporate plans. Frequently those who lead and help lead major companies fail to develop specific *personal* goals and plans. Some do not have a Personal Mission Statement. They may think about their long-range goals, or the actions they need to take in order to reach those goals, but they never really make it an official plan. However, those people who have a written plan have incredible success in achieving their goals.

> *"If you don't design your own life plan, chances are you'll*
> *fall into someone else's plan. And guess what they have*
> *planned for you? Not much."*
> Jim Rohn[8]

During most of the 1980's, I was responsible for the strategic planning of a major multi-million dollar corporate division, but it never occurred to me that I should have a written plan for my personal life. In 1995, when I developed my own Personal Mission Statement, I realized that my life was inconsistent with my mission statement. It was clear that some changes should be made, and the process of examining my life led to the development of a Life Plan.

Just as our Family Trip West had many purposes, so too does a Life Plan:

- To help you develop meaning and direction for your life.
- To encourage you to make good decisions.
- To help you build your life on proven life principles.
- To help you establish goals for your life.
- To identify what you want and need out of life.
- To identify what you hope to accomplish in life.
- To help you make the most of every opportunity life has to offer.

What is a Life Plan?

If you've never developed a Life Plan, examined your life goals, or established life priorities, This Handbook will help you do that. When it comes to achieving goals, the greatest adversaries are apathy, inertia, and just plain laziness. We all have a tendency to just keep doing what we have always been doing and if there is no crisis, then there is no reason to do anything different.

Unless you commit to doing something new, nothing new will happen. If you have nothing to commit to, then you can be assured nothing different will occur. Good intentions are not enough. But you can get discouraged if you focus on overwhelming goals. Therefore, we will break down goals and priorities into small steps that can be achieved. We encourage you to begin by thinking short-term. Begin by concentrating on today, next week, or next month. Let next year take care of itself.

"One step at a time" is always great advice. Most of us spend too much time and energy focusing on the one thing we cannot control – the result. We must allow the result to come after we have put energy into traveling the road. We cannot control the outcome, all we can do is control the road we are traveling and keep our eye on the destination.

Our job is to know the destination, make a plan to get there, focus on doing the right things for the right reasons, and not worry about our success or failure. A failed attempt to do something is not failing.

Failing is not trying.

Focus on the Future

Our primary focus will be on the future. Although we can learn much from the past, we assume that you will automatically integrate your past experience into your current thinking as you begin looking at goals and objectives. If you have unresolved issues in your past, we hope that you will find strength and encouragement in looking to the future. Recognize, however, that dealing with some issues of the past may require professional help. If that is your situation, we encourage you to take the necessary steps to find a professional counselor to help you.

Focus on the Right Things

I have always remembered a simple statement that provides real insight into human behavior and response: "If you think you can or can't, you're right." That statement indicates the importance of thinking about the right kinds of things, in the right way, and with the right understanding.

Planning Subjects and Categories

In order to make this study practical we have chosen nine planning categories we believe represent the major areas of life that should be addressed. Obviously there are other categories or sub-categories that might be developed. If you are interested in other subjects, simply use the process and the concepts provided here to address other categories or subjects.

Truth

Because of widespread beliefs in society today, we must pause to define the word "truth." It has become fashionable today to reject the idea of "absolute truth" in favor of "relative truth." In his book, *Right from Wrong,* Josh McDowell explains what he calls the "seismic shift" from absolute to relative truth.

> At one time children were raised in an atmosphere that communicated absolute standards for behavior: certain things were right and certain things were wrong. . . . At one time, our

society, by and large, explained the universe, humanity, and the
purpose of life from the Judeo-Christian tradition: a belief that
truth existed, and everyone could know and understand it. A
clear understanding of what was right and wrong gave society a
moral standard by which to measure crime, punishment, ethics,
community values, character, and social conduct. It became the
lens through which society viewed law, science, art, and politics
– the whole of culture.

In the last several decades that concept has changed drastically.
Our children are being raised in a society that has largely
rejected the notions of truth and morality, a society that has
somewhere lost the ability to decide what is true and what is
right. Truth has become a matter of taste and morality has been
replaced by individual preference.[9]

Many people accept this world view, called *relativism,* that McDowell
described. It is the view widely promoted by film, by TV, and by much of
secular education. Much of society holds this view. Our parents may
have taught us this world view, but even if they didn't, we probably have
absorbed at least some of it by a sort of "cultural osmosis." Today, many
people label "absolute truth" as "intolerance."

The problem with relativism is that it is based on the values of men. If
we accept faulty values as "truth," then our understanding will be faulty,
resulting in desires, goals, actions, and plans that are inconsistent with
what is best for our lives.

How do _you_ define "truth"?

Incidentally, if there are children in your present or your future, you
already know, or will soon find out, that "truth" will become an
important concept in raising them.

We accept and adopt the traditional definitions of right, wrong, good,
and bad in this book. We will spend no time debating whether
something is right, wrong, good, or bad.

The Strategy

We will work on the plan one step at a time and then bring it together at the end with action steps to achieve your goals. Those action steps will be focused on the goals and objectives you desire for your life. You can attack or implement a small portion at a time, gain success, and then move on.

We will _not_ attack the plan as a whole. It's the same strategy as the person that wants to eat an elephant: one bite at a time.

Why Bother?

Why do this?

You should do this because you care and want to make changes or improvements in your life. Or you may want to get a handle on life from a broader perspective. You may feel that you have no control over where your life is going. If you're not sure where you are going, you could end up anywhere!

Your Life Plan will:

- create focus and attention on what you deem is important,

- cause you to take action,

- reduce distractions and hindrances, and

- create desire and motivation.

The End Result – What Can I Expect?

After examining your current life, identifying your life values, and setting major life goals based on your life priorities, you will develop action steps to accomplish some of your goals.

At that point you must simply decide to do it! We will provide tools and ideas for you to make the implementation easier. If you want help we can also provide coaching assistance. For more details on our assistance go to Chapter 15.

Most of us have never done any kind of extensive self-examination and have certainly not thought about writing down our plans. I can tell you personally there is much to be gained from writing down your objectives rather than just thinking, talking, or meditating about them. It will give you a clear picture of your life and help you evaluate what you really want to accomplish.

Life planning is not a difficult process. It will certainly be easier for those who have thought about these questions before. Some of you might even have an existing plan of some kind. If so, this will be a good tool to check on where you are and how you are doing. If you have such a plan, it would be worthwhile pulling it out as you progress through the remaining parts of this book.

"If you don't know where you're going, any path will get you there!"

I don't know the source of this quote but I have had it emblazoned in my brain since my college days. I think it came from one of my business textbooks. I have heard it repeated a number of times over the years, primarily because it is so true. If you don't know your destination, then any choice of roads at all the forks in life will be an acceptable choice. It won't really matter which road you take because you don't have a destination in mind anyway. And when you get there you won't know you have arrived.

We need a purpose, a destination, and priorities so we are not wandering aimlessly through life. Even if you are not organized or a "planning person," be assured we will walk you through every step. Knowing your path is important because:

1. Every path leads somewhere.

2. The life-road on which you are traveling, the direction in which you are heading, and your expected destination will determine how you live your life.

3. You cannot allow apathy, other people, or chance to determine either your path or your destination.

Without purpose and direction it is difficult to make good choices. Just thinking about the questions in the following process will be helpful.

You should also be aware of the tools in the Appendices for additional help in developing or implementing your plan:

A. Spiritual (Christian Perspective)

B. Prioritizing

C. Scheduling

D. Decision-making

REMINDER: If you are a Christian, read Appendix A before you continue.

Chapter 2

Consequences

Mess with the bull and one usually gets the horns.
Latin American saying[10]

General

Consequences are a vital concept in our understanding of making good choices and setting goals to have a successful life. You have complete freedom to choose what you want to do. But you cannot choose the consequences. Thus, it is important to manage and control our actions because the result of poor choices could be a disaster.

You and I will bear the consequences of our words and actions. It is like a law of nature. My wife drilled this concept into our kids. If she said it once she said it a thousand times, "Your actions all have consequences." And, when she said it, the kids knew there was no "eventually" involved.

If you don't want to endure the negative results of poor decisions, think in advance what your actions are likely to produce. What you do and what you say will have lasting impact on others and on yourself.

There Will be Consequences

Life is a series of decisions and choices. We are constantly making choices about both significant and insignificant situations. The advice above is a good example of the importance of consequences. Choices shape the course of our lives. Some people learn a great deal from the consequences of their actions and others seem oblivious and never learn anything.

You may hear people claim that their actions do not have consequences. This is absolutely not true. Consequences are real and can produce both good and bad results. Our goal is to help you make better choices so the consequences are positive rather than negative.

Physical consequences are a law of nature. If you touch a hot stove you will get burned. If you walk into the street in front of a truck you will be injured. Behaviors have predictable consequences as well. If you cheat and lie, people will stop doing business with you and your reputation will suffer. If you are not dependable, people will learn not to trust you.

We know of a person who had surgery and was told not to walk on his repaired knee. He ignored the doctor's orders and hobbled around on crutches anyway. He lost his balance, fell through a glass door, and received additional injuries. He blamed the doctor for an outcome that was clearly the consequence of his own poor choice.

By definition consequences occur as a result of something else happening. They are the outcome of some other action. The result may occur immediately or it could take a while, even years. This is often one of the reasons that we make poor choices – the consequence does not occur immediately and because of this we think there will never be consequences. We cannot allow this delay to persuade us that consequences don't happen.

The actual consequences you experience will vary depending on your circumstances, but there will be consequences nonetheless. The degree or size of the consequence will also vary, but we should not be fooled into thinking small transgressions are insignificant. Even seemingly small acts can produce significant consequences.

"One who steals has no right to complain if he is robbed."
Aesop[11]

The Slacker

There was a farmer who had been plowing hard for many days with an ox and mule yoked together. The ox told the mule that they should pretend to be sick and rest. The mule declined saying, "No, we must get the work done, for the season is short." But the ox played sick and the farmer brought him hay and corn and made him comfortable.

When the mule came in from plowing the ox asked how things had gone. The mule said, "We didn't get as much done but we did okay, I guess." The ox asked, "Did the old man say anything about me?" Nothing," said the mule. The next day the ox played sick again. When the tired mule came in he asked again how it went. "All right, but we sure didn't get much done." The ox asked, "What did the old man say about me?" The mule replied, "Nothing directly to me, but he had a long talk with the butcher."[12]

This is similar to the message in the old story concerning the consequences of a hearty breakfast to the chicken and the pig. A breakfast of ham and eggs to the chicken is a temporary inconvenience, but to the pig it is a permanent and lasting consequence – it's a real commitment.

You will need to make a real commitment in order to claim honesty, integrity, and truth as core values in your life. You may find it tempting to be lazy, particularly if no one is looking over your shoulder. However, sooner or later that behavior will catch up with you.

I chose the word "slacker" because it means someone who avoids his work or obligations. The synonyms for slacker may surprise you: no-account, vagrant, good-for-nothing, and bum. If you tend to get a little lazy with your undertakings, remember the ox in this story. The projected destination for the ox was not a desirable result. You cannot afford to be a slacker or apathetic when it comes to how well you are going to live your life.

All actions have consequences!

Count the Cost

There is a saying that indicates we all will ultimately be invited to a party where we will dine on our own consequences. Whether your actions were wise or unwise, you will eventually bear the consequences. Thus, it is important to think about the consequences in advance and count the cost. What will result from your words or actions?

If you don't want to endure the negative results of poor choices, think in advance what your actions are likely to produce. What will you say when co-workers urge you to join them at the local bar every night before you go home? What will you say if someone makes a sexual advance or lurid remark? What will you do or say if you are offered some form of drug? What will you do or say if someone who has been drinking offers you a ride home?

Regardless of the particular situation, it will always be easier to arrive at a positive outcome if you have thought ahead, evaluated the circumstances, and determined in advance how you will respond to these types of situations.

What you do and say in questionable circumstances will have a lasting impact on your life. This truth is almost as important as understanding that the world is round and not flat. Emblazon the following truth in your mind and on your heart:

> *Consequences shape lives.*
> *Choices produce consequences*
> *which direct the course of life.*
> *Therefore, count the cost!*

Envy

The Oxford Dictionary describes envy as a feeling of discontented or resentful longing aroused by someone else's possessions, qualities, luck, or situation. Envy is not an attractive attribute. You may think the grass is greener in that other field but it may not be as attractive as you think. Buddha has said:

"Do not overrate what you have received, nor envy others.
He who envies others does not obtain peace of mind."
Buddha[13]

There is no purpose or peace in envy. Coveting the things of others, whether they are material objects, mental abilities, or acquired skills, will not produce anything worthwhile. Honoré de Balzac has said, "Envy is the most stupid of vices, for there is no single advantage to be gained from it."[14] He is absolutely right! I challenge you to think of a positive attribute of envy.

Consider the following questions:

- Why do you want it? Is it something you need or simply want?

- Envy implies jealousy, covetousness, and resentment. Which of these is driving your envy?

- If you acquire the object of your envy, what are you going to do with it? Why?

It is certainly appropriate to admire people of character and status. It is also appropriate to desire and copy their good habits and character traits. But that's not envy. Determine what you want and define your goals in terms of what you want your life to be. Don't waste time resenting or desiring that what your neighbor has.

Legacy

Our words and actions can have impact for a long time. The ongoing impact of poor behavior is a concept that escapes many people. Poor decisions can affect a family for many generations. Parental behavior establishes a pattern that becomes the blueprint for a child's future behavior. For example, parents who frequently lie are modeling lying as an acceptable way to avoid responsibility, inherently teaching their children that lying and deception are acceptable ways of behaving.

These things children experience in their home become their normal response. What is witnessed by small children is later reproduced. They can learn to be trustworthy, reliable, and dependable, or they can learn to do drugs, smoke, and gossip. What a child sees modeled in the home becomes the normal response, and that behavior cycle often continues into future generations.

> ***Your actions, both good and bad, establish the foundation of your life, lifestyle, and legacy.***

Your legacy extends into future generations; therefore, be sure that it is a positive one! Most people have no concept of how their behavior can impact the future. This is dramatically illustrated by examining the stories of Jonathan Edwards and Max Jukes.

Jonathan Edwards was a Puritan preacher in the 1700s. His descendants demonstrate the powerful influence of wise choices and a godly life. At the turn of the 20th century, A. E. Winship decided to trace the descendants of Jonathan Edwards and compare them to a man known as Max Jukes.

Mr. Jukes was incarcerated in the New York prison system at the time Jonathan Edwards was preaching. Winship found that 42 of the men in the New York prison system could trace their heritage back to Max Jukes. Jukes, an atheist, lived a godless life. He married an ungodly woman, and from the descendants of this union 310 died as paupers, 150 were criminals, 7 were murderers, and more than half of the women were prostitutes.

In contrast, the record of Jonathan Edwards' progeny tells a much different story. An investigation of 1,394 known descendants of Jonathan Edwards revealed

- 13 college presidents,
- 65 college professors,
- 3 United States Senators,
- 30 judges,
- 100 lawyers,
- 60 physicians,
- 75 army and navy officers,

- 100 preachers and missionaries,
- 60 authors of prominence,
- 1 Vice-President of the United States,
- 80 public officials in other capacities,
- 295 college graduates, among whom were governors of states and ministers to foreign countries.

Today, instead of the blessings like those that came to Jonathan Edwards' progeny, we are seeing a growing multitude like the descendants of Max Jukes! Have you seen a family in which the grandfather was an alcoholic – and his sons and grandsons abuse alcohol, too? Have you seen a family plagued with sickness, drug abuse, debt, poverty? Often that is because someone did not make good choices. We are going to leave a legacy for our children and grandchildren. Will we pass on a blessing or a curse?[14.5]

If you want to leave a legacy, impact someone's life.

How to Spend Your Life

Lysa Terkeurst in her book, *The Best Yes,* says this about making decisions: "The decision you make determines the schedule you keep. The schedule you keep determines the life you live. And how you live your life determines how you spend your soul."[15]

Think about that statement. You could say this truth in a number of ways – Ms. Terkeurst chose this particular description. But any way you say it the meaning is, *your decisions determine your life*. The consequences of your decisions constitute your day and your future. You are always living in the midst of the choices you make, so, make good choices. The consequences will determine how you live your life, or in Terkeurst's words, "spend your soul."

How do you want to spend your soul?

It's Not Fair

Unfortunately, life is not fair. Worrying about fairness, arguing about it, or fighting it will be of little value. Being "fair" generally means that everyone is treated equally (the concept of socialism). The issue of something being fair often tends to become more important to us when it impacts us personally. When something touches us directly, we become concerned about fairness.

But life is not fair!

If you believe that life is intended to be fair, then it's not "fair" to others less fortunate that you were born in America and are therefore privileged. It is not fair that you have avoided poverty, wars, terrorism, natural disasters, tyrants, dying in an accident, abuse . . . .

It's unrealistic to argue it's not fair that we experience the consequences of our poor choices, especially since we are the ones making those poor choices. If we think we shouldn't incur the result of our poor choices then we certainly should not expect to experience the rewards of our good choices. We must accept the fact that life is not necessarily fair and that "bad things do happen to good people."

Obviously, things happen to us that are completely random or out of our control. We can't control weather disasters, traffic accidents, or illness. We can reduce the chances of those problems by taking precautions when bad weather threatens, by driving carefully, and by making heathy choices. But we can't eliminate them all. In the end, we control what we can by making good choices and understand that some things in life simply are not fair.

Think about the consequences,
then choose wisely!

Who to Blame

Blame is a big concern for many people today. When something bad happens, the first reaction by many is to find someone to blame. Many people no longer accept the concept of an "accident." It's become the norm to assign blame and "make someone pay." We have forgotten the definition of an accident: an unplanned or unforeseen occurrence. It is no longer acceptable to merely restore the victim to their position before an accident. Rather we think we must extract a huge monetary punishment from the other party.

Some of us react in illogical ways to consequences. The most illogical is people who totally ignores the obvious dangers of what they are about to do and then, rather than accepting the consequences, cast blame. They become angry or embarrassed and attempt to find someone or something to blame in order to take the attention off their own poor judgment.

Taking responsibility for mistakes, errors, misunderstandings, or accidents is becoming a lost art because many children have been raised to believe they do not need to suffer consequences. If the result of some action is not good or right, they expect someone else will fix it and the boss, parent, or coach has no right to hold them responsible.

Admitting mistakes and taking responsibility is a characteristic of those who are living their best life.

Mistakes

What happens when we make a mistake? A mistake is not the end of the world – it's a mistake, not a death sentence! If we make a wrong choice, we must rethink the issue and select another path. We all make mistakes. The real challenge in life is how we handle those mistakes.

Statistics say that successful entrepreneurs on the average have seven failed business ventures before they finally succeed. What does this tell us? If something is not working or the desired result is not occurring, stop and change direction. Try something new.

Not every choice we make will be the right decision. Expect a few failures in life and don't be overwhelmed if what you do does not work out as you expect. If the choice was bad, wrong, or ill-advised, fix it!

Pride will often cause us to hide mistakes.

Unintended Consequences

No one intentionally makes bad choices. We may think about a choice and simply not understand the consequences. In reality, however, we may be overlooking the consequences because of our desire to follow a certain course of action.

Regardless of the reason, unintended or poor results sometimes occur. However, there are ways we can reduce the probability of negative results and increase the probability of positive results. Here are five tips you could adopt before making decisions:

1. **LOOK (THINK)** before you leap!

   Take time to consider the consequences.
   Ask yourself, "What would 'wisdom' do?"
   Think logically.

2. **LISTEN** to the advice of others.

   Seek out trusted friends.
   Remember, however, others may have their own agenda.

3. **CONSIDER** the pros and cons.

   How will this decision impact me or others?
   Will I be proud of the outcome?
   What would my mother think?

4. BE PATIENT.

"Sleep on it" is often excellent advice.
Research as much as you can.

5. EMOTIONS often cause poor decisions.

Base your choices on facts and reality.
Do not make decisions based on your emotions.
Emotions can have disastrous impact on decisions.

*"It is the peculiar quality of a fool to perceive
the faults of others and to forget his own."*
Cicero[16]

Chapter 3

Life Analysis

Know yourself.

General

The objective of this Life Analysis chapter is to survey your life situation for information that will be used in later chapters to identify your core values, life priorities, commitments, and goals. That will help you develop action steps to achieve your goals and ultimately live a better life.

If you have already read and completed the Life Analysis in one of the books from the Life Planning Series, the questions and exercises are generally the same, but your answers here will be focused on your total life, not on just on a particular life principle. However, some of your responses will be the same or similar and it would certainly be helpful to have that book handy as you complete this Life Analysis.

The Approach

Before you begin the work of drafting a Life Plan, we believe it's necessary to review and identify your skills, talents, strengths, and weaknesses. What are you good at? What do you do poorly? What do you struggle with? What are you like? What do you like to do? What are your gifts, talents, attributes, characteristics, and experiences?

Most people already have an inherent sense of their skills, talents, and gifts. Our objective in this section is for you to recognize those talents, skills, gifts, and your character so that your Life Plan will build on your strengths while helping you understand and address your weaknesses.

We want to help you look specifically at these areas of your life in order to bring them into sharper focus as you begin to think about your core values, priorities, and goals in life.

Life Analysis – Know Yourself

The first step in any form of life planning is to know and understand where you are today. So, the first objective will be to identify your present situation and circumstances. What is your current situation? What is impacting your decisions and ultimately your life today? Before we begin, take note of the following suggestions:

1. During this process you may find that you draw a blank on a particular question. If that happens, move on to the next question and return to the unanswered questions later.

2. If the question doesn't apply to you for some reason, leave it blank and move on.

3. You might find it convenient to write your initial responses in a separate notebook or on your computer. Modify your initial drafts to accurately reflect your thoughts and circumstances and then transfer them into this book. Regardless of how you develop your answers, keep your notes, as they may be useful at a later date.

Grab your favorite beverage and let's begin!

KNOW YOURSELF – Interests

INSTRUCTION: What are the things and activities you love to do? What gives you joy?

1.
_____

2.
_____

3.
_____

4.
_____

5.
_____

6.
_____

7.
_____

8.
_____

KNOW YOURSELF – Skills

INSTRUCTION: Check the following items that you believe represent significant skills or talents in your life. This list isn't comprehensive. It's just to get you started thinking. Use the blanks to fill in other significant skills or talents.

__ Communication	__ Electronics	__ Judgment
__ Writing	__ Building	__ Creativity
__ Speaking	__ Fixing things	__ Music
__ Financial planning	__ Coordinating	__ Art
__ Accumulating wealth	__ Planning, Organizing	__ Drama
__ Analyzing	__ Motivating others	__ Composition
__ Research	__ Performance	__ Mathematics
__ Leadership	__ Persuasiveness	__ Social Media
__ Computers	__ Selling	_____
__ Technical	__ Intelligence	_____
__ Parenting	__ Scholarship	_____

INSTRUCTION: Based on the above, describe in a little more detail your _most important_ skills and abilities?

1.

_____

2.

_____

3.

_____

4.

_____

5.

_____

6.

_____

KNOW YOURSELF – Strengths

INSTRUCTION: What are your <u>other</u> strengths, special skills, and passions?

1. _____

2. _____

3. _____

4. _____

5. _____

6. _____

7. _____

8. _____

KNOW YOURSELF – Weaknesses

INSTRUCTION: What are your weaknesses?

1. _____

2. _____

3. _____

4. _____

5. _____

6. _____

7. _____

8. _____

KNOW YOURSELF – Reputation

INSTRUCTION: What is your reputation today? What do others think of you? What do others respect, appreciate, or admire about you? Alternatively, what characteristics might bother them about you? How would others describe you? If you have good friends and a thick skin, you might survey a few of your inner circle and get their feedback.

1. _____

2. _____

3. _____

4. _____

5. _____

6. _____

7. _____

8. _____

KNOW YOURSELF – Roadblocks

Who or what things do you fear the most? What are the roadblocks, distractions, and hindrances that might prevent you from improving your life in any way? Circle any that might apply and add your own in the empty boxes.

Time	Failure	Bankruptcy	Divorce	Death
Public speaking	Confrontation	War	Loss of friends	Loss of job
Poor health	My boss	Guilt	No legacy	God
Disabilities	Apathy	Relationships	Peer pressure	Family
Inability to stand firm	Immoral behavior	Unethical behavior	Lack of skills/abilities	Emotions feelings
Fears and insecurities	Improper motives	Lack of core values	Lack of patience	Lack of purpose
Bad habits				

INSTRUCTION: Based on what you circled above, record any <u>serious</u> roadblocks or hindrances that could prevent you from living a better life. Indicate the reason you believe they are roadblocks.

1. _____

2. _____

3. _____

4. _____

5. _____

6. _____

KNOW YOURSELF – Character

How would you evaluate your personal character? Do you have any serious character flaws? If you do, you may need to deal with them separately in order to make real progress toward living a better life.

INSTRUCTION: Circle the positive traits which you lack and the existence of character flaws that might hinder you.

LACK OF POSITIVE CHARACTER TRAITS:				
Honesty	Kindness	Caring	Forgiving	Goodness
Hopeful	Humility	Dependable	Loving	Diligence
Respectful	Godly	Patient	Generous	Satisfied
Peace	Merciful	Trustworthy	Self-controlled	Thankful
Devout	Disciplined	Obedient	Gentle	Prudent
Sincerity	Fair/Just	Grateful		

EXISTING CHARACTER FLAWS:				
Bad language	Boastfulness	Gossip	Slanderous	Lying
Cheating	Stubbornness	Anger	Hostility	Deceitfulness
Foolishness	Mischievousness	Rebellion	Hypocrisy	Envy
Unruliness	Ingratitude	Pride	Immorality	Addictions
Jealousy	Bitterness	Hatred	Unforgiveness	Shame
Respect	Fear	Deceit/Fraud	Vanity	Revenge

The above list is not exhaustive. If you think of other issues, enter them in the empty boxes.

INSTRUCTION: Review the issues you have identified and list anything below that could <u>seriously</u> hinder achieving a better life. List the issue and how it would negatively impact your ability to achieve your objectives.

1. _____

   _____

2. _____

   _____

3. _____

   _____

4. _____

   _____

KNOW YOURSELF – Legacy

We've all gone to funerals and listened to eulogies. Eulogies usually contain complimentary comments about the deceased – sometimes we might even think we're at the wrong funeral, because that's not how we remember that person!

Take a moment and think about the following question: "What will be said about me when I die?" It's not our intent to be morbid, but just realistic. If I want people to remember me as kind, then I may need to adjust my behavior so that will happen. I need to consider what I'm doing – or should be doing – to cause others to see me that way. If I want my business associates to see honesty and integrity, then my behavior, my actions, and my talk must reflect those characteristics.

INSTRUCTION: Answer the following questions.

1. What is it that you are doing, can do, or would like to do that would cause others to say, "That was a life well-lived"?

_____

_____

_____

_____

_____

_____

2. If you were to write your own epitaph, what would you say?

_____

_____

_____

_____

_____

_____

3. What would you like to overhear a friend or an acquaintance say about you?

_____

_____

_____

_____

_____

_____

KNOW YOURSELF – Defining Life Experiences

We want your focus in this book to be on the future. But it is very important that you note where you have been before you map out where you are going. Our strengths, weaknesses, character, needs, and wants are often a product of our defining life experiences. As we look into the future and begin to define our goals, it's important that we recognize the events and occurrences that have shaped our lives. While for this purpose we want to examine only the major defining life experiences, we recognize that all experience will impact our lives.

We have listed below descriptive words that will trigger the memory of potential defining experiences in your life. Given the description, fill in the experience in your life that best fits that description. Just identify the event; no explanation is necessary. Although some of the words are similar, they may trigger remembering different experiences in your life. You will not have something to fillin on every blank.

DEFINITION: A defining life experience is one that impacted your life in a substantial way and altered the way you lived or acted. Examples might include: marriage, birth of children, job/career, death, divorce, addiction, salvation, education, leaving home, relocation, vocation, care of aging parent, loss or acquisition of a friend, change in health, etc.

	High Point Peak Triumph	Low Point Valley Failure	Turning Point Life Change Transforming Experience
Character			
Community			
Education			
Spiritual			
Family			
Work/Career			
Relationships			
Financial			
Health			
_____			
_____			

INSTRUCTION: After completing the table above, circle the 2 to 4 items that you believe have had or will have the most profound impact _on your future_. For each of those events, write a short statement defining the _positive_ influence you want that event to have on your life in the future:

(1)

_____

_____

(2)

_____

_____

(3)

_____

_____

(4)

_____

_____

NOTE: If one of the above events is a negative experience and you currently do not see how it can be a positive influence, simply list that event and do not attempt to write a statement.

KNOW YOURSELF – Dreams

INSTRUCTION: What are your dreams for your future? What are your passions? What does a better life look like? What do you think will bring you great joy?

1. _____

2. _____

3. _____

4. _____

5. _____

6. _____

KNOW YOURSELF – Other

INSTRUCTION: What is important about you that has not been noted above? Have you missed anything important about your family, career, community, church, health, education, relationships, finances, spiritual condition, recreation, pleasure, social media, skills, abilities, or character? List and describe any issue that would impact your ability to live your best life.

1. _____

2. _____

3. _____

4. _____

5. _____

6. _____

KNOW YOURSELF – Conclusion

This concludes your information gathering. You should now have a good overview of who you are and what might impact your ability to make progress toward significant changes in your life.

The next step in the process of knowing yourself is to use this information to determine your core values, life priorities, and your personal mission statement.

> *"Wisdom is to live in the present, plan for the future,*
> *and profit from the past."*
> Unknown[17]

REMINDER: If you are a Christian you should skip ahead and develop your Personal Mission Statement before you identify your core values in the next chapter. See Appendix A for details.

Chapter 4

Life Values – Core Values

"The problem with most leaders today is they don't stand for anything. If you don't stand for anything, you'll fall for anything."
Don Shula[18]

General

What are the standards by which you live? What values do you cherish? What do you believe in? What values or standards will you absolutely not compromise or violate? The latter are your core values.

Self-assessment and full understanding of yourself and your environment must begin with identifying and knowing your core values. Core values are the principles, standards, or beliefs that are so important to you that you would not violate them. They will dictate your most important decisions and help you choose your direction.

You don't need to have your whole life figured out, but you do need to know what matters most to you. You need to know your ethical and moral standards. What issues or actions do you believe in so strongly that you would be ashamed if you violated them? These are values and principles you believe in and live by, and to the best of your ability you will not forsake them. They represent who you really are. They are your core values.

If you are a religious person you might have a core value that indicates you would stand firm on your religious principles, and you might name them. If you love and seek intellectual improvement, you might have a core value related to seeking and gaining knowledge and wisdom. If you are a dedicated parent, you probably have core values related to your children or parenting. Core values may change or become more or less important as you age and the path of your life journey changes.

We are not suggesting that you have a core value on every major subject; only what has particular significance for you today. You may be aware of several of your core values but you probably have never written them down. This exercise will be an important step in understanding what is important to you.

If this is a new subject for you, you might start by looking at some typical subjects like attitude, gratitude, integrity, health/fitness, work ethic, diligence, self-control, anger, money/wealth, immorality, reputation, violence, courage, mercy/compassion, self-confidence, perseverance, patience, curiosity, and generosity.

There are other subjects that might be appropriate for you to consider; for example: wisdom, influence, leadership, safety/security, indebtedness, family, parenting, humor, volunteer service, ethics, joy, relationships, moderation, balance, justice/injustice, addictions, laws, and nature of career work.

Your core values should be on the topics that are <u>very</u> important to <u>you</u>. For example, you might have a financial core value of: "I will never spend more than I earn. I will pay off credit cards monthly."

Good Advice

> *Watch your thoughts; they become words.*
> *Watch your words; they become actions.*
> *Watch your actions; they become habits.*
> *Watch your habits; they become character;*
> *Watch your character; it becomes your destiny.*
> Unknown[19]

Take a minute and read the above several times and then think about your destiny. What is determining your destiny? Do you need to change any of your words, actions, habits, or character traits?

Core Values

Develop your values based on a total life perspective and make them work for you. If you have never thought about this before, we recommend you begin with 5 to 8, but no more than 12. This is a critical step in this planning exercise, so spend sufficient time thinking and evaluating your final choices. Remember, core values are those values, beliefs, or standards that you will absolutely not compromise or violate.

INSTRUCTION: Develop your list of core values and record them here. We suggest you try to list twelve and then cut the list back to the best 5 to 8.

1. _____

2. _____

3. _____

4. _____

5. _____

6. _____

7. _____

8. _____

9. _____

10. _____

11. _____

12. _____

Do any of the core values you listed above relate to honesty or integrity? How about any of the other <u>primary</u> Life Principles: friends, speech, diligence, and money? If not, do you need one? You may not, but we believe that these are the cornerstones of living a better life. If you ever have times when these values are called into question, you should seriously consider a core value in this area.

"There are three constants in life...
change, choice, and principles."
Stephen Covey[20]

Chapter 5

Personal Mission Statement (Preliminary)

"Have a clear plan or strategy to translate your success philosophy into desired results. Adopt an effective work ethic, with a laser-focus and requisite execution strategies to produce results. "
Archibald Marwizi[21]

Introduction

In this chapter we will begin the work of developing a preliminary *Personal Mission Statement*. You could describe it as your life purpose.

A Personal Mission Statement is a general statement aimed at identifying your primary purpose in life. It is the rationale or justification for your existence. It may indicate the activities you intend to perform, the kind of person you want to be, or a major goal you want to accomplish. It defines what you want your life to be about.

Your Personal Mission Statement acts as a plumb line. A plumb line is a weighted line that a bricklayer holds up against a wall to make sure the wall is perfectly square. The bricklayer knows that the smallest deviation at the foundation of the wall will cause major problems as the wall is built and formed. He knows that he can't just "eyeball" it and end up with a strong, useful, and beautiful wall.

Your Mission Statement is the standard against which all goals and actions should be evaluated. If you have an important decision in front of you, one of the first questions to ask is, "Does this fit within my personal mission?" An analogy from the construction industry may be helpful in describing the purpose of a personal mission statement.

If you think of your life as a brick wall, your Personal Mission Statement is your foundational plumb line. You can hold it up and measure everything you do against it. You can look at each choice and decision in life against this plumb line and see if that choice or decision will help the wall go up straight and in the direction it's supposed to go, or if it will cause a deviation that doesn't fit with the design you have in mind. Deviations weaken the wall and crooked walls may ultimately fail.

Therefore, before we look closely at specific goals and objectives you want to accomplish, it is important to establish this foundational plumb line: your Personal Mission Statement. You want your core values, priorities, commitments, and goals to be consistent with your Mission Statement. In Chapter 9, after you have developed and evaluated goals in certain areas of your life, we'll finalize your Personal Mission Statement. That's why we are referring to the mission statement in this chapter as "preliminary."

What should be included in your Personal Mission Statement? How broad in scope should it be? It could include:

     1. reasons you exist; a rationale and justification,

     2. activities or functions you want to perform,

     3. the kind of person you wish to be,

     4. a vision of what you want to become, or

     5. what you want to achieve in life.

Your Personal Mission Statement need not include all these points, but it should certainly address several of them in some way. The focus of your statement should be long-term, which might be 15 to 20 years, not the next 5 years. Think in terms of your life in total.

The Approach

Before you begin drafting your Personal Mission Statement, you should review Chapters 3 and 4, where you recorded your skills, talents, character, legacy, defining life experiences, and core values. We each have a different combination of these characteristics and experiences.

Our objective in Chapter 3 was for you to recognize who you are in order that your Life Plan be built on your strengths, while helping you understand and address your weaknesses.

We want you to look specifically at these areas of your life in order to bring them into sharper focus as you begin to think about your objectives and particularly your life mission.

First Draft

Using the information you developed in Chapters 3-4, draft your own _preliminary_ Personal Mission Statement, considering such things as:

- What do you want to accomplish?

- What kind of person do you want to be?

- How do you want to use your skills and abilities?

It would be a good idea to do this in pencil! This is a working statement, and it won't say what you want it to say on your first several tries. Look back at the things you've done in Chapters 3-4 and how you want to be remembered. It won't necessarily sound polished the first time. Try to include everything you think is important initially; you can eliminate excess words and thoughts when you begin to review and edit.

_____
_____
_____
_____
_____
_____
_____
_____
_____

If you feel you need additional guidance in drafting this initial statement, you may wish to focus on one or more of the following concepts:

- How will you use your gifts, talents, or skills?

- What type of steward will you be with your time, talents, skills, and resources?

- Where does your job, career, or vocation fit into your life priorities?

- What do you want to accomplish in life?

- How will you use your wealth?

- What type of parent or spouse do you want to be?

One way to start is to choose the two or three major subjects that apply to your life and write down what you want to accomplish in that area at the end of your life.

Revised Drafts

Now edit your first draft. Try to keep it between 15 to 30 words – the shorter, the better! Ideally it would be short enough that you could easily remember and repeat it. My personal statement is eleven words which makes it easy to remember. You may come back to this again and again, each time changing it and getting it closer to what you want as you proceed through the remaining chapters.

We suggest that you continue to use a pencil, for both practical and psychological reasons! A pencil says, "I can change this thing any time I want!"

(1st)

_____
_____
_____
_____
_____
_____

(2nd)

_____
_____
_____
_____
_____
_____

(3rd)

_____
_____
_____
_____
_____
_____

(4th)

_____
_____
_____
_____
_____
_____

Chapter 6

LIFE PRIORITIES

Set priorities that make the main thing, the main thing!

Priorities

What are the things that are very important to you <u>today</u>? What are your life priorities? Where do you <u>currently</u> spend your money and your time? What do you spend your life doing and thinking about? For this initial list of priorities, ignore anything new that you may be considering relative to living a better life. Record just your life priorities <u>today</u> (the good and the bad).

If you do something daily or regularly, then it is probably a priority. If you average more than an hour a day doing something, it's also probably a priority. What do you regularly spend money on? Assuming you have a normal 8:00 – 5:00 job, what do you do in the evenings and on weekends? If you spend an hour at the bar before you come home each night, that's a priority. If you go to the gym most days, that's a priority.

You might have priorities related to your spiritual life, education, the ethical standards of your friends, your health and diet, hobbies and activities, raising your children, your marriage, your times of pleasure and relaxation, politics, volunteer service, your work ethic, saving money, immorality, your job or career, where you will live, and your personal growth.

INSTRUCTION: What are your actual top 8 to 15 life priorities <u>today</u>? Simply answer the question, "What is important to me <u>today</u> based on how I spend my time and money?"

1.

_____

2.

_____

3.

_____

4.

_____

5.

_____

6.

_____

7.

_____

8.

_____

9.

_____

10.

_____

11.

_____

12.

_____

13.

_____

14.

_____

15.

_____

NEW ISSUES – URGENCY:
If you learned that you had only two years of life left, what impact
would that have on your Life Priorities? How would they change?

_____

_____

_____

NEW ISSUES – SACRIFICES AND RISKS:
What <u>new</u> risks or sacrifices would you have to make in order to live a
better life? Would that change your Life Priorities? How?

_____

_____

_____

_____

NEW ISSUES – KNOWING YOURSELF:
Review your "Life Analysis – Know Yourself" and "Core Values" and
determine if there is anything new that should change or be added your
Life Priorities.

_____

_____

_____

NEW ISSUES – LIVING A BETTER LIFE:
Given a desire to live a better life, what <u>new priorities</u> would you need
to adopt? Ask yourself what you must absolutely do in order to be
successful. What new priorities does that create and how would any
existing priorities have to change?

_____

_____

_____

_____

Final Life Priorities

Prepare a list below of your new and revised Life Priorities. Try to keep this list at 6 to 8, but no more than 12.

1.

_____

2.

_____

3.

_____

4.

_____

5.

_____

6.

_____

7.

_____

8.

_____

9.

_____

10.

_____

11.

_____

12.

_____

Chapter 7

Life Commitments

"There's a difference between interest and commitment.
When you are interested in doing something,
you do it only when it's convenient.
When you're committed to something,
you accept no excuses, only results."
Kenneth Blanchard[22]

General

Thinking about Life Commitments is an important exercise for many before beginning to identify Life Goals. At this stage in the planning process we have identified our Core Values, preliminary Personal Mission Statement, and Life Priorities.

Life Commitments are those commitments that must be made in order to achieve your Personal Mission and Life Priorities. In many cases the difference between a goal and a commitment might be rather small or blurred; thus, it's a good way to begin thinking about Life Goals. What commitments must you make in order to accomplish your desired legacy, dreams, Core Values, Life Priorities, and ultimately your Life Mission.

If you want to be a diligent and hard worker, you might need to commit to working at the same pace whether the boss is present or not. If you have friends and associates who are pulling you down, you may have to commit to finding new friends. If you want a better job or career, you may have to commit to certain education objectives. If you have a priority to love your family unconditionally, you may have to commit to guarding your speech.

Existing Commitments

INSTRUCTION: List any commitments that already exist in your life because of your present circumstances. For example, you may be committed to caring for a sick relative, or taking care of a child who is not your own. Maybe you are already dealing with self-control issues and you have committed to controlling your anger. Record here the commitments you already have in your life.

1.

_____

2.

_____

3.

_____

4.

_____

5.

_____

6.

_____

New Life Commitments

Are these the same as your Life Priorities? No! Your Priorities identify the _things that are very important_ to you, while your Life Commitments are _things you must do_ to make your Life Priorities a reality in your life.

Life Commitments are sometimes particularly useful if they focus on areas where you have particular difficulties.

It's likely that you will need to make new commitments to accomplish your Core Values and Life Priorities. For example, if your desire is to be honest, you will also have to commit to being trustworthy, dependable, reliable, and loyal. If you want to be generous, then you can't love money. If you desire to guard your speech, you cannot be out of control and let anger control your tongue. If you are going to live free of drugs, you must commit to eliminating friends and associates who use drugs.

The point of these examples is to demonstrate that if you are serious about living a better life, then there will be commitments necessary for you to be successful. Try to make your commitments specific enough that they will be useful to you.

Since your Life Priorities inherently identify your objectives, examine those priorities and determine the related commitments that you must make in order to achieve each Life Priority. The focus should be on what you must commit to in order to achieve a better life. Do the same thing with your Core Values and preliminary Mission Statement. Think about what traits, behaviors, activities, or habits must be managed or controlled in order for you to achieve your objectives.

Final Life Commitments

INSTRUCTION: Based on the above, develop the Life Commitments you believe are necessary for you to successfully live a better life. These should be significant commitments; therefore, select the 4 to 8 that would really help you in living a better life.

1.

_____

_____

2.

_____

_____

3.

_____

_____

4.

_____

_____

5.

_____

_____

6.

_____

_____

7.

_____

_____

8.

_____

_____

*"My philosophy of life is that if we make up our mind
what we are going to make of our lives,
then work hard toward that goal,
we never lose – somehow we win out."*
Ronald Reagan[23]

Chapter 8.0

GOALS – Introduction

"Your ability to discipline yourself to set clear goals,
and then to work toward them every day, will do more
to guarantee your success than any other single factor."
Brian Tracy[24]

General

In this chapter we will develop the goals you need to establish in order to achieve a better life. There are nine categories:

1. Life Principles and Character Attributes

2. Habits

3. Friends and Family Relationships

4. Work and Work Ethic

5. Education

6. Community Service

7. Money and Wealth

8. Health

9. Spiritual

Choose Your Categories

At this point you have a decision to make as to how you want to proceed. You have two options:

> A. You could develop goals for all nine categories.

> B. You could choose to prepare goals for only some of the categories, in which case you would choose the most important. You might arbitrarily decide to work on only 4 or 5 categories.

Recommendation

Develop at least one goal in each category. Then when it is time to prepare action steps, and you want to proceed more slowly, prepare action steps for only the most important goals that will make significant change in your life.

Choose the Number of Goals in Each Category

Again, you have two choices:

> A. You could decide you want only one goal per category, or

> B. You could decide to develop all the important goals within the categories.

Recognize that you might have some categories with only minor goals and other categories that have several very important goals. If there is an important goal in any category, make sure you record it.

RECOMMENDATION: We suggest you choose option (B) above. Identify all the important goals within all the categories in which you are working, then choose all the important ones, even if half of them come from the same category.

A Category Does Not Apply

If there is a category in which you have little or no activity, just skip it.

There's an Important Category Missing

If you want to add another category, either use the space where there is a category that does not apply, or use a separate notebook to record the appropriate information.

What is a Typical Life Goal?

Generally, life goals are serious, relatively large, and important objectives you want to achieve in life. You would need to accomplish these goals to live the life you desire. Following are some examples we provide to set the tone and give you some perspective on what life goals might include.

1. To know right from wrong and stand firmly on my core values.

2. To utilize effectively the wisdom, skills and gifts I possess, particularly _____, in order to _____.

3. To speak with wisdom and tact.
    Throughout history many intelligent people were ineffective because they didn't combine their knowledge with tact. Tact allows us to communicate wisely what intelligent thought produces.

4. To know when to confront others and when to back off.

5. To be trustworthy – I will not compromise my integrity.

6. To be loyal and faithful to my family, friends, and employer.

7. To be humble and live my life with gratitude.

8. To be honest – no exceptions.

9. To obtain the education and training necessary to work as a _____.

*"Life takes on meaning when you become motivated,
set goals and charge ahead after them in an unstoppable manner."*
Les Brown[25]

Chapter 8.1

LIFE PLANNING PRINCIPLES

*"Life is ten percent what happens to you
and ninety percent how you respond to it."*
Lou Holtz[26]

If you haven't read any of the books in the Life Planning Series you may not be familiar with the title of this chapter. The Life Planning Principles are the focus of the book series and represent the principles one might choose to adopt if they wanted to live a better life.

LIFE PLANNING SERIES

It is our objective in the Life Planning Series to help the reader choose the best path and give them tools to make good decisions in their life journey. The series is divided into five different categories to help organize the books and make it easy to find related subjects.

These subjects and Life Principles are perfect candidates for your Life Goals, particularly the Life Principles. Below is a table listing the subjects and the Life Principles of the series.

Subjects		Life Principle
Personal Character:		
Integrity*	honesty, truth, compromise/standing firm, justice, fairness	Be honest, live with integrity, and base Life on truth.
Reputation	respect, responsibility, sincerity	Earn the respect of others.
Leadership	power, decisiveness, courage, influence, loyalty	Lead well and be a loyal follower.
Identity/Self-Image	humor, being genuine, authenticity, confidence	Be confident in who you are.
Wisdom	discernment, correction, folly, foolishness	Seek knowledge, understanding, and wisdom.
Personal Relationships:		
Friends*	Friends, associates, acquaintances	Choose your friends wisely.
Family	Honor, parenting, discipline	Honor your family.
Love	Love is . . .	Love one another.
Compassion	humility, mercy, goodness, kindness	Treat others as you would want to be treated.
Forgiveness	reject grudges and revenge	Forgive others; do not hold grudges or take revenge.
Self-Control:		
Speech*		Guard your speech.
Anger	self-control, self-discipline, patience	Always be under control.
Addiction	moderation, life balance	Live a life of balance and moderation, not excess.
Immorality	temptation	Set high moral standards.
Work Ethic:		
Diligence*	apathy, laziness, perseverance, resilience, energy	Be diligent and a hard worker.

Trustworthiness	dependability, reliability, responsibility	Be trustworthy, dependable, and reliable.
Skills	curiosity, knowledge, education, abilities	Seek excellence; strive to do everything well.
Wealth:		
Money*	wealth, poverty	Do not love money or worship wealth.
Gratitude	generosity, thankfulness, gratefulness	Be thankful, grateful, and generous.
*The first subject listed under each of the categories above make up the Primary Life Principles.		

There are certainly other important attributes that you might think of. For example you might want to have a goal related to your thought life, specific moral standards, dress code and appearance, righteousness, goodness and kindness, knowledge, understanding and wisdom, sin, standing firm, self-examination, self-sufficiency, being zealous, thought life, or having goals and a plan.

PLANNING CATEGORY #1 – Life Principles and Attributes

Guidelines for drafting Goal Statements:

1. They should be general and long-term in nature.
2. They should create some focus and direction for your life.
3. They should indicate what you want to achieve in this area.
4. They might indicate what kind of person you want to be.

Examples of Possible Goal Statements:

Integrity: I will be honest, live with integrity, and base my life on truth.
Friends: I will choose my friends carefully.
Speech: I will choose my words carefully.
Diligence: I will be a diligent and hard worker.
Money: I will not love money or worship wealth.

Intentionality: I will have a plan, and know where I am going.

Thought Life: I will intentionally filter what I read and see in order
to control the subject matter of my thoughts.

Draft Your Goal Statements

INSTRUCTION: Review the table and suggestions above, particularly the Life Principles. Determine if any of these topics represent potential Life Goals for you. If so, write out the goals you may want to adopt below:

Draft your own goals for the category of LIFE PRINCIPLES and ATTRIBUTES.

_____
_____
_____
_____
_____
_____
_____
_____
_____
_____
_____
_____
_____
_____
_____
_____

"Life isn't about finding yourself.
Life is about creating yourself."
George Bernard Shaw[27]

Chapter 8.2

Habits

"You do not write your life with words...You write it with actions.
What you think is not important. It is only important what you do."
Martin Luther King Jr.[28]

Habits

Following is a list of about 40 habits in six categories. Review this list to determine if you have any of these habits and if they are candidates for your Life Goals.

RELATIONSHIPS	Don't get angry; be in control	Allow others to help you	Value the time of others; be punctual
	Associate with good, smart, kind, caring people; choose friends wisely	Guard your speech; no cursing; use gentle, loving, caring, and kind words	Affirm and compliment others
	Be socially active; network; have friends	Spend quality time together as family	Eat dinner together as a family; don't eat alone
ATTITUDE	Be positive	Smile and be happy;	Ask questions; be curious
	Don't give up easily; be tenacious; persevere	Be an overcomer; don't let problems derail you	Be gracious and thankful
	Be a self-starter	Be positive; glass half-full	Embrace change

FINANCIAL	Be frugal; spend less than make; pay off all credit card debt monthly;	Save money; but don't hoard	Live comfortably within means
BE ACTIVE	Engage in stimulating and enjoyable hobby or activity	Read for pleasure and edification	Volunteer time, talent, and resources; be generous
	Participate in art and music	Seek knowledge	Live a balanced life
ORGANIZED	Know when to say no; don't over commit	Think through decisions; don't make choices off the top of your head	Set daily, monthly and yearly goals
	Plan your day	Prioritize	Journal
HEALTH	Have fun, enjoy yourself	Balanced diet; healthy eating	Rest, relax, vacation
	Spend time in nature; be outdoors	Laugh; enjoy humor; laugh at yourself	Sleep well and exercise

PLANNING CATEGORY #2 – Habits

Guidelines for drafting your Goal Statements:
1. They should be general and long-term in nature.
2. They should create some focus and direction for your life
3. They should indicate what you want to achieve in this area.
4. They might indicate what kind of person you want to be.

Examples of Possible Goal Statements:

Debt: I will pay off all credit card debt monthly.
Family: I will spend quality time with my family each day.
Decisions: I will not make major family decisions without
                  discussing them with my family.

I Will Encourage Others:
      1. I will encourage others at work by _____.
      2. I will encourage my spouse by _____.
      3. I will encourage my parents by _____.
      4. I will encourage my friends by _____.

Draft Your Goal Statements

INSTRUCTION: Review the material above, and determine if any of these topics represent potential Life Goals for you. If so, write out the goals you may want to adopt below:

Draft your own one or more goals for the category of HABITS.

_____

_____

_____

_____

_____

_____

_____

_____

_____

_____

_____

_____

_____

_____

"Repetition of the same thought or physical action develops into a habit which, repeated frequently enough, becomes an automatic reflex."
Norman Vincent Peale[29]

Chapter 8.3

Relationships

"Life isn't about finding yourself.
Life is about creating yourself."
George Bernard Shaw[30]

General

There are a number of categories of relationships: family, friends, co-workers, associates, clients, customers, acquaintances, advisors, and mentors. We will mostly address the first two, but you can develop goals for any of these categories, depending on your circumstances.

Your personal relationships are a very important aspect of living a better life. Other people constitute a large portion of time in our lives after work and family. The choice of your friends and how you manage relationships will influence to a great extent how you spend your time. Nurturing relationships will have a major impact on your ability to achieve a better life, because in many cases your family and friends are living it along with you.

"The better you are at surrounding yourself with people of
high potential, the greater your chance of success."
John C. Maxwell[31]

There are many attractive attributes you need in relationships, but the most important may be *trust*. You must be loyal to your family and friends in order to maintain good relationships.

Family, friends and acquaintances have great influence over how you spend your time and what you think and talk about, which will determine what you do. Thus, if you think and talk about drinking, drugs, and wild parties, that's what you're likely to do. It's human nature. The people you associate with can lead you down paths where you don't want to go.

The obvious conclusion is that you must nurture your family relationships well and choose friends carefully. You may have to eliminate friends that do not share your core values and interests.

You need people of high character in your relationships. They must have standards or core values similar to your own or a lasting relationship is normally not possible. For example, if both parties do not have similar views about truth-telling, it will be very hard to maintain much of a relationship if one of the parties is frequently telling lies and cannot be trusted. Family and real friends should be absolutely truthful with each other, even when the truth hurts.

Relationships can be damaged beyond repair by poor personal character traits. Once a relationship is seriously damaged, it is often very difficult to repair. We must be vigilant in making decisions that would not hurt or betray our family and personal relationships.

We need meaningful relationships with the people around us in order to live healthy and productive lives. Outside the community that automatically exists in our families, your circle of friends, associates, and acquaintances can be your life support, particularly if normal family relationships do not exist.

Tonny Rutakirwa has said, "No matter whether you believe this or not, your friends command a major proportion of your destiny; they contribute largely to your future."[32]

Choose the right friends and
keep yourself around like-minded people.

Advice About Your Conversations

1. BE QUICK TO LISTEN AND SLOW TO SPEAK

There is no advantage to speaking up first in a conversation. However, there are some advantages to being slow to speak. You are likely to appear wise and discerning, rather than foolish, because you will have had time to thoughtfully consider what you want to say. You are less likely to be wrong and demonstrate your ignorance or foolishness. A well-thought-out response is likely to be recognized as sound advice. An answer or comment based on some thought will not be an emotional reaction but information that can improve, advance, and lift up the conversation.

2. DON'T GRUMBLE AND COMPLAIN

No one likes to be around a person who is always grumbling and complaining. Someone who is positive, friendly, and pleasant is far more desirable company. Positive people tend to look on the bright side of things. They can be contagious, but so can unpleasant people.

3. DON'T QUARREL AND ARGUE

Quarrels are likely to create animosity among friends and associates. If animosity is the result of quarreling over a subject or question that cannot be won, that argument is not worth pursuing. Have you ever won an argument or won someone to your side by quarreling? I certainly have not. Prolonged conflict and rebellion accomplish nothing. Quarrelsome people have few friends. It is far better to simply avoid conflict and rebellion because they will lead to serious problems in both personal and business relationships.

4. TALK LESS AND LISTEN MORE

Listening means that I pay attention to someone in order to understand what they are saying and meaning. I listen with thoughtful attention.

Thus, I am able to respond to the questions or issues being raised, and I do not speak about something else that is on my own agenda.

Those who do not listen will often create problems for themselves because they are not responding correctly or they are not doing what was asked. Poor listeners are often in trouble and suffer the consequences of bad decisions. Their unsatisfactory response is often because they did not listen well.

Be intentional about listening. Here are three tips that will help:

- Don't listen to judge others or their comments and opinions.

- Be patient. Allow others to finish. Don't interrupt.

- Respond to what is being said by others. Don't change the subject. Listen to what others say so that you are not duplicating what was said before you.

Husbands, Wives, and Children

All relationships, not just marriage, are to be based on the foundational concept of loving one another as ourselves, submitting to one another in love, being kind and compassionate to one another, forgiving each other, and living in harmony with one another. Marriage partners should treat each other with consideration and respect. Both partners should display good character, wisdom, generosity, and respect for each other.

Your family relationships must receive top billing in your desire to cultivate good relationships. Love and child-rearing are part of our commitment and many of us, perhaps most of us, fall short in doing what is required.

Children scrutinize everything we do as parents. Because our actions speak so louder than our words, we demonstrate our true values far more through our walk than our talk. Our children, as well as all those we interact with, must see that we live out what we say we believe. To believe others are unaware of contradictions between our words and actions is the height of foolishness. We urge you to demonstrate to others, and especially your children, the type of behavior you expect in return. Your children will mirror what you do and say.

Consider what you are demonstrating to others by your:

personal habits	community service	treatment of your family
spending practices	language	driving
choice of movies	choice of friends	attitude about God
choice of books	voting habits	attitude toward your job
possessions	choice of TV programs	use of social media
leisure activities	attitude toward life	attitude toward laws
charitable giving	value system	

attitude toward people of different race, color, culture, religion, etc.

Based on the list above, make a mental note of your actions, behaviors, lifestyles that you believe most influence others. Then list the three that you think are your best and your worst:

BEST	WORST
1.	1.
2.	2.
3.	3.

PLANNING CATEGORY #3 – Relationships

Guidelines for drafting your Goal Statements:

1. They should be general and long-term in nature.
2. They should create some focus and direction for your life
3. They should indicate what you want to achieve in this area.
4. They might indicate what kind of person you want to be.

Examples of Possible Goal Statements:

Friends: I will choose my friends and associates wisely.
Fools: I will not allow foolish people into my circle of friends.
                 I will be very cautious in following their advice.
Children   I will teach my children to be generous and charitable
                 by setting a good example.

Children: I will teach my children good character, right and wrong, and compassion for others.

Children: I will encourage my children to maximize both their physical and intellectual skills and abilities.

Family: I will intentionally build strong family, marriage, and parental relationships through love, compassion, and protection.

Parents: I will respect and honor my parents.

Faithful: I will be faithful and trustworthy in all my personal relationships. I will keep all my promises, especially my marriage vows.

Role Model: I will be a role model in all my relationships, exhibiting to the best of my ability love, forgiveness, compassion, and especially grace.

Respect: I will display respect for others, for the elderly, for property, and for the laws of our country in all my relationships.

Perspective: I will reach out and try to make a friend of a person of different_____ to help me better understand their views and feelings.

Discrimination: I will do my best to fight the evils of racial, cultural, and economic discrimination.

Draft Your Goal Statements

INSTRUCTION: Review the material above, and determine if any of these topics represent potential Life Goals for you. If so, write out the goals you may want to adopt below:

Draft your own one or more goals for the category of RELATIONSHIPS.

_____

_____

_____

_____

_____

_____

_____

_____

Chapter 8.4

Work

"Today is life – the only life you are sure of.
Make the most of today. Get interested in something.
Shake yourself awake. Develop a hobby.
Let the winds of enthusiasm sweep through you.
Live today with gusto."
Dale Carnegie[33]

General

Your work matters and you should find satisfaction in your work. What kind of work are we talking about? Obviously we include the work you do for pay: your job, career, part-time work, and temporary jobs. We also include necessary work around the home that is done by husband, wife, and children. For many, this is a career, and although they receive no salary or direct compensation for their time, it most certainly is work.

Attitude Toward Work

Unfortunately, many people do not have a high view of work. Some well-known and respected people have said:

Robert Frost: "By working faithfully 8 hours a day, you may get to be a boss and work 12 hours a day."

Abraham Lincoln: "My father taught me to work, he didn't teach me to love it."

Unfortunately, some very negative attitudes and habits have developed in the workplace. The quotes from Frost and Lincoln are just the tip of the iceberg. Attitudes like this can be devastating in the work environment.

Solomon was a wise, wealthy, and influential king. He wrote about work and said, *"I know that there is nothing better for men than to be happy and do good while they live. That everyone may eat and drink, and find satisfaction in all his toil . . ."*[34]

> *"The price of success is hard work, dedication to the job at hand, and the determination that whether we win or lose, we have applied the best of ourselves to the task at hand."*
>
> Vince Lombardi[35]

Many of today's workers do not share Solomon's view of work. Let's briefly examine some attitudes of typical workers.

1. Who Cares?

Many workers are bored with their responsibilities, bored with the people they work with, and bored with life in general. Although the media often paints a picture of excitement, high finance, and great accomplishments occurring in offices and manufacturing plants all across our land, the truth is that for many workers, the daily work experience is "just a job" and its only value is monetary.

2. It's My Number One Priority!

At the other end of the spectrum are those who believe that work determines self-worth. For these people work, career, and advancement are the core of life. Everything important revolves around work, power, success, and earnings. Achievement on the job controls how they act and who they are. It defines them. A successful career is their ultimate goal in life and all other areas of life such as family, relationships, religion, and health are subordinate to the career goal.

Over-involvement in a career has, historically, been a particular problem for _men_. Today, however, career-oriented women are lured into the same trap. For many workers, the job:

- defines their life,
- demonstrates their success,
- delineates their self-image,
- is their primary source of peer recognition,
- illustrates their character,
- provides their feeling of fulfillment, and
- determines whether or not they consider themselves successful!

This is a sad but true summary of many career-driven people! It is as important for spouses, friends, and co-workers to understand this environment as it is for the workers to understand it in themselves.

3. Ethics

Issues of morality and integrity confront us in every line of work. Some are universal, such as cheating the employer out of time, effort, or money. Pilfering is rampant in some businesses and industries. Other issues of morality or ethics are more specific, for example:

- Movie and television producers who crank out endless sex and violence, ignoring the destructive influence on children, teens, and adults;
- Lawyers who are more concerned with what is technically legal than what is just;
- Doctors who devote themselves exclusively to lucrative practices, while the poor are without medical care;
- Politicians who blindly follow the instructions of their party and financial benefactors, ignoring the needs of society;

- Professors who care more about their publishing career or tenure than their students;
- Store owners and clerks who sell liquor, cigarettes, and pornography to minors;
- Manufacturers who produce inferior or dangerous products.

Sadly, the list could go on and on.

What Should be the Case?

We should all expect joy and satisfaction from our work. Sincerity and diligence should be rewarded. Obedience to the employer's wishes should be expected and followed. Employees should work to the best of their ability.

The employer should expect and receive an honest day's work. Stealing is more than just taking "things" from an employer. Those who give less than a full day's labor for a full day's pay are also stealing. Employers can also steal from employees by paying less than a fair wage.

Dishonesty should not be rewarded. Lying and cheating will lead to disaster and should be punished. Most employers will fire cheating and dishonest employees. The employer has a right to receive the employee's very best and has an obligation to pay fairly for that work.

Employees should be industrious. They should not need someone to oversee their work for it to be done well and on time. They should be diligent, hard-working, and industrious, not lazy or shiftless. They must remember that poor or careless work can affect others in many ways.

What is Your Work Situation?

- Do you find purpose and meaning in your work or are you bored?

- Are you challenged by the implications of maintaining your integrity in your work?

- Are you finding joy and satisfaction in your work?

If you are struggling with any of these questions, we suggest that you take a serious look at your goals and make a concerted effort in one or two areas to make improvement. Don't try to address all the issues at one time: take it one step at a time!

PLANNING CATEGORY #4 – WORK

Guidelines for drafting your Overall Goal Statements:

1. They should be general and long-term in nature.
2. They should create some focus and direction for your life
3. They should indicate what you want to achieve in this area.
4. They might indicate what kind of person you want to be.

Examples of Possible Goal Statements:

Attitude: I will do my work diligently and with perseverance, no matter what the level of work or my responsibility.

Fair Value: I will work honestly, giving a full honest day's work to my employer, no matter what my pay or compensation.

Full Value: I will do my share of work, not leaving my responsibilities for others to do or fix. I will do my work to the very best of my ability, performing my responsibilities beyond that required or expected by my employer.

Purpose: One goal of my work is to provide for the needs of others who are less fortunate.

Satisfaction: I will perform my work with an attitude and approach that will bring satisfaction to myself, my employer, and my family.

As Employer: I will deal honestly and fairly with all employees, treating them with respect and dignity.

Legitimate: I will only do work that is morally legitimate.

Integrity: I will uphold honesty and integrity in the manner of my
               work, not compromising my standards in any work
               related activity.

Satisfaction: I will make the most of my talents, skills, and gifts
                in order to maximize job performance and satisfaction.

Draft Your Goal Statements

INSTRUCTION: Review the material above, and determine if any of these
topics represent potential Life Goals for you. If so, write out the goals
you may want to adopt below:

Draft your own one or more goals for the category of WORK.

_____

_____

_____

_____

_____

_____

_____

_____

_____

"The dictionary is the only place that success comes before work.
Work is the key to success, and hard work can help
you accomplish anything."
Vince Lombardi[36]

Chapter 8.5

Education

*Developing a plan will address the need for education.
If you want to be a secretary then you need to learn the skills
of a secretary. If your lack of education, skill, or knowledge is creating
part of your problem, then the simple answer is to get educated.*

General

Education is often the key to success in many areas of life. In this chapter we are not talking about basic public education that is needed by everyone. Our reference to education means practical education in order to perform special physical or mental skills.

You might obtain this education from a local educational institution, from your parents or friends, or you might develop this skill from training on a job location. To seek and pursue knowledge, wisdom, skills, and abilities is a significant step toward optimizing your job satisfaction.

Don't let anyone tell you that you are not smart enough, strong enough, or young enough to learn a new skill. It all comes down to your desire and determination.

Possible Situations

Consider the following examples and note the goal statements that might apply to your life:

Formal Education:

    Elementary through High School

        I will complete my high school education or its equivalent.

        I will apply myself to achieve the grades I need to go to college.

        I will graduate in the top ___% of my class.

    College Education

        I will graduate from college with a degree in _____.

        I will graduate in the top ___% of my class.

    Practical/Vocational Training

        I will go to vocational school and learn to be a _____.

    Continuing Education

        I will _____.

Personal Growth:

        I will read _____ new books each month on the subject of _____.

        I will take up the hobby of _____ in order to learn the skill of ____.

        I will take on a part-time job in order to learn how to _____.

        I will find a friend or mentor who can teach me how to _____.

PLANNING CATEGORY #5 – Education

Guidelines for drafting your Goal Statements:

1. They should be general and long-term in nature.
2. They should create some focus and direction for your life
3. They should indicate what you want to achieve in this area.
4. They might indicate what kind of person you want to be.

Examples of Possible Goal Statements:

Formal Education: I will pursue all necessary education requirements in order to become a ____.

Vocational Skills: I will complete all training requirements to become a _____.

Search: I will investigate the requirements for becoming a _____ and determine if I want to make a job/career change.

Apprentice: I will find someone in my field of interest and try to be hired on as a part-time apprentice to determine if the work is appealing and satisfying.

Draft Your Goal Statements

INSTRUCTION: Review all the material above and determine if any of these topics represent potential Life Goals for you. If so, write out the goals you may want to adopt below:

Draft your own one or more goals for the category of EDUCATION.

_____
_____
_____
_____
_____
_____
_____
_____
_____

"Anyone who stops learning is old, whether at twenty or eighty.
Anyone who keeps learning stays young.
The greatest thing in life is to keep your mind young."
Henry Ford[36.5]

Chapter 8.6

Community Service

"The purpose of human life is to serve,
and to show compassion and the will to help others."
Albert Schweitzer[37]

General

Community service can mean different things to different people. In this book we mean the act of volunteering time, talent, and resources to help other people or organizations provide goods or services to those that are less fortunate. This is volunteer work that is done without pay.

Some may refer to this as charitable work. We are referring to it as community service because the expectation is that you are actively doing something in your local community. If all you are doing is giving money to a national charity, that is not community service for the purposes of this book.

In fact, simply giving money to a local organization to be spent in the local community is not community service by our definition.

Opportunities for Service

There is a great need for service to the many single parents in our society. If you have a heart for children or want to serve in this special way, consider volunteering to help single parents. Could you start a program so high school mothers can finish school? Could you rock babies in a hospital nursery? Could you start or volunteer in a Latch Key program in your public school district so children have a place to go after school? Is there a younger mother or father in your neighborhood you could mentor? Could you teach English as a second language to non-English speaking families in your community? Could you go the grocery for an elderly or shut-in neighbor?

What do you like to do and how could you use that to benefit the people in your neighborhood or community? Could you mentor or advise people or businesses based on your skills and abilities? Could you volunteer at a local food bank?

Use your creativity to find a way to help someone. If you want to leave a legacy then change someone's life. You can do that with simple acts of kindness or by just sitting with someone who needs companionship.

The Needy

Those less fortunate than you could use your help. Not only do they need your help, you will be blessed for helping them. How many people have you heard say that they received more from providing help than the one they helped? We exist to help the needy and poor. They will always be with us.

Could you volunteer at a local organization that provides food, clothing or shelter to those in need? Could you assist the elderly, such as home repair and mowing? You may not have to look further than someone in your neighborhood. Those who give mercy and compassion receive compassion in return. Who do you know that needs your help?

Maybe your help could be in the nature of helping the disadvantaged who are being oppressed. Can you help them be treated fairly and with dignity? Do you have special training or skills that you could use to help others who could not afford such services?

PLANNING CATEGORY #6 – Community Service

Guidelines for drafting your Goal Statements:

1. They should be general and long-term in nature.

2. They should create some focus and direction for your life.

3. They should indicate what you want to achieve in this area.

4. They might indicate what kind of person you want to be.

Examples of Possible Goal Statements:

General: I will love my neighbors as myself.
Volunteer: I will volunteer at the local _____.
Specific: I will provide my time, talents, and resources to
                help _____.
Needy: I will help the needy by _____ .

Draft Your Goal Statements

INSTRUCTION: Review the material above, and determine if any of these topics represent potential Life Goals for you. If so, write out the goals you may want to adopt below:

Draft one or more goals for the category of COMMUNITY SERVICE.

_____
_____
_____
_____
_____
_____
_____
_____
_____
_____
_____
_____
_____
_____

*"I am of the opinion
that my life belongs to the community,
and as long as I live,
it is my privilege
to do for it whatever I can."*
George Bernard Shaw[38]

Chapter 8.7

Wealth and Finances

"Wisdom is to live in the present,
plan for the future and profit from the past."
Unknown[39]

Introduction

Because of the dangers and temptations associated with money and wealth, it's important that you establish a set of financial values and guidelines regarding:

- how you think about money,

- the importance you attach to money, and

- how you spend money (what you do with it).

It is clear from historical evidence that money and wealth create many temptations. Money can destroy families, relationships, marriages, and business partnerships.

It's of paramount importance that you control your money and wealth and that it does not control you.

We will provide more help and assistance in this section because money has traditionally been a difficult area for most people to control.

General Guidelines about Money

In what or whom do you put your financial hope and trust? Is it in your family? Is it in a financial advisor? Or, is it in yourself because you are successful or prosperous?

Here are six guidelines to consider:

1. We should not love money.
2. We should not allow luxury to lead to self-indulgence.
3. We should use our material possessions to help those in need.
4. We should not be eager to get rich.
5. We should not accumulate wealth for ourselves or our heirs.
6. We should be content with what we have.

One danger in being wealthy – or even financially "comfortable" – is that money tends to have too great of an importance in our lives. This often results in wrong or dangerous attitudes. Our priorities can become distorted and we can become too concerned about material things.

Wealth can make us believe that we are better than others. Do you know people who equate success in their life with wealth?

Where are your priorities?

Let's look more closely at the first three of the above guidelines.

Love of Money:

A life that revolves around the amount and value of possessions leaves no room for anything else. Because the possession of money tends to make us believe that we do not need the help of anyone else in our lives, we become self-sufficient and self-reliant. "Just look at what I have been able to do on my own! I don't need any help from anyone."

Why does this happen? Because money, which often goes hand-in-hand with success, easy living, pleasure, satisfaction, and earthly gratification, gives us a false sense of our own self-importance. I repeat, "*a false sense of our own self-importance.*"

Money can be a stumbling block for many of us. Those whose main goal in life is to accumulate wealth often sacrifice everything else in order to achieve that goal. They may even go against what they thought were their core values. The _love_ of money is at the root of all kinds of evil. Remember, it's not the money itself, it's the love of money.

Self-indulgence:

Money can be a significant hindrance to living a better life. Your lifestyle should not be extravagant or too luxurious, but instead discreet, moderate, self-controlled, and not wasteful. Remember, the warnings about money are not against money itself but against its misuse.

What treasures are you storing up? Why? Are your financial priorities in line with living a better life? How important is money to you? Does it control you? Does your spending reflect a grateful life or a selfish life?

Helping the Needy:

Help the needy! This is easy to say, but often hard to do. It's very easy to be generous if you have a gift for helping others. The problem for many of us is that we don't have a heart for being generous or helping others financially. Therefore, if helping others financially does not come naturally we have to be intentional.

Being generous often comes down to the question of whether we are being good stewards of what we possess. Helping the needy is an inherent part of what one does in living a successful life.

How to Avoid the Dangers of Money

Your lifestyle should not be extravagant or overly luxurious, but you need not deprive yourself of rewards and extras. Simply use good judgment. Live comfortably but seek ways you can use your money to have a positive influence on others. The following six suggestions will help you avoid the dangers that money and wealth may create, as well as provide advice on improving your financial stewardship.

1. Life Priorities

What should I do with wealth beyond my basic needs? How can I be honorable in the way I handle my money? How much do I need for necessities and how can I best use what is left over? Do I have a clear picture of what are necessities and what are not?

What are your financial priorities?

2. Prudent lifestyle

Do not wear yourself out getting rich in order to buy a bigger house or more luxuries. Develop financial wisdom in order to show restraint. Living on credit has become a way of life for many in our society. Debt can become a deep pit of financial disaster. Some manage to crawl out of the pit by themselves. Others do so only with professional help. How can you avoid this bottomless pit?

> a. Learn to distinguish the difference between what you need and what you want. We may think we need a new car. Upon careful consideration, however, we may come to realize that what we need is dependable transportation, and that "new car" is a want, not a need. Our options may include repairing our current car, looking for an affordable used car, or using public transportation. Wants and needs are _not_ the same thing. Learn to distinguish between them.

> b. Avoid impulse buying on credit and develop financial patience. We really don't like to wait for what we want! We love instant gratification, and credit cards encourage us to indulge this love. Debt makes it easy to fall into a "see it – like it – buy it" reaction mode.

> c. Be sure you understand how much interest you pay on your credit card bills. This alone should be enough to encourage limiting your indebtedness!

> d. Never charge items you will consume. You will be paying for years on things long since used up.

e. Be wary of using credit to buy luxuries you currently can't afford. These luxuries may include such things as cars, boats, a larger home, vacations, etc. You must live within your income. The spending of your friends should not influence your spending. Be willing to say, "We really can't afford that right now." Teach your children that instant gratification is not a healthy lifestyle.

3. Be careful about indebtedness:

Indebtedness can be both good and bad. Debt is just like many other things in life: if you do it in moderation there is no problem, but if it gets out of control your life can suffer. There are situations in which indebtedness is necessary – very few people can buy a house without acquiring a mortgage! It's obvious, however, that we should not incur more debt than we can handle.

One of the biggest problems of indebtedness is not the debt itself, but the stress and tension that such debt creates. It becomes a point of contention, worry, and concern for you, your family, and for those who may provide you collateral or security.

In general, it is wise to avoid debt as much as possible and use credit with caution.

4. Avoid excessive financial risk:

Incurring excessive debt is an act of irresponsibility and can lead to bankruptcy or poverty. The prudent see danger and take refuge from excessive debt, but the fool keeps going and suffers for it. It is much wiser to diversify and reduce risk, not build it up.

Exercise particular caution in assuming responsibility for another person's debts (e.g., co-signing loan agreements). Endangering your future for something outside your control is a risk that should be undertaken only if you totally understand your risk and can afford the loss of the entire amount. This can be an especially tricky problem when the debt involves someone in your family.

5. Plan for retirement:

Prudent planning in the area of retirement is far more important today than it was only a few years ago. People are living longer and certain costs such as long-term health care are unknown. The ultimate future of Social Security and Medicare is in question. We cannot assume that others will take care of us or that someone (the government) is obligated to provide for our needs.

6. Don't Gamble:

In the past organized gambling was available only in casinos in only a very few locations. Now, in many states, we can gamble at our local grocery store through state sanctioned lotteries. The entry of state governments has put a face of legitimacy on gambling, but it is still gambling. Today there is the exploding sports gambling phenomena. You can download an app on your phone and gamble away anything you desire.

Gambling itself presents some inherent problems:

> a. it promotes and legitimizes greed and materialism;
> b. it takes resources from more important and essential needs;
> c. it can be addictive;
> d. it can be perceived as a solution to financial problems;
> e. it appeals to and promotes the criminal side of society; and
> f. it exploits the weaknesses of our human character.

We must conclude that gambling is not an attractive pleasure, but rather a guilty pleasure. It produces negative results for those who participate.

Taking Stock – Practical Applications

Let's look at some very practical financial issues. What do you believe and what do you actually do? These statements are designed to help you think about your financial values and your actual practices. If you believe in the stated practice then your actions should match your stated beliefs.

SPENDING:
I believe it is appropriate to live within my income, so I regularly spend less than I earn.

SAVINGS:
I believe I should save money regularly, so I routinely put money into saving or investment accounts.

RETIREMENT:
I believe it is appropriate to save for retirement, so I contribute to an IRA or employer savings account.

CREDIT CARDS:
I believe that debt and credit cards can create stress and financial temptations, so I always pay off my credit card balance each month.

BUDGETING:
I believe in the need for personal budgeting, so I have a budget and review it regularly.

INVESTING:
I believe in taking only appropriate financial risk, so I practice caution in my investments.

Again, do you agree with these concepts and do your actions confirm your belief? The question you should ask is, "Are my practices consistent with my beliefs?"

You will want to consider carefully those practices and actions that are not consistent.

PLANNING CATEGORY #7 – Wealth

Guidelines for drafting your Goal Statements:

1. They should be general and long-term in nature.
2. They should create some focus and direction for your life
3. They should indicate what you want to achieve in this area.
4. They might indicate what kind of person you want to be.

Examples of Possible Goal Statements

Debt: I will live debt-free, borrowing only in limited circumstances.
I will repay all debt promptly, striving to be debt-free by _____.
I will pay off all credit card balances in full every month.
I will go into debt only to purchase a home or business.

Lifestyle: I will live a moderate lifestyle, consistent with my income, using any excess for retirement and for the special needs of others less fortunate.

Means: I will live within my means and not spend more than I earn.

Risk: I will limit my debt and the financial risk I undertake.

Inheritance: I will use my excess for helping others in need today and limit the amount to be accumulated for heirs.

Spending: I will save _____% of my salary every month, and spend the remainder on material needs.

Wealth Accumulation: I will accumulate adequate wealth to fund retirement and use the excess to _____.

Draft Your Goal Statements

INSTRUCTION: Review the material above, and determine if any of these topics represent potential Life Goals for you. If so, write out the goals you may want to adopt below:

Draft your own one or more goals for the category of WEALTH

_____

_____

_____

_____

_____

_____

_____

_____

_____

_____

"If we command our wealth, we shall be rich and free;
if our wealth commands us, we are poor indeed."
Edmund Burke[40]

"Money cannot buy peace of mind. It cannot heal ruptured
relationships, or build meaning into a life that has none."
Richard M. DeVos[41]

"Too many people spend money they haven't earned,
to buy things they don't want,
to impress people that they don't like."
Will Rogers[42]

Chapter 8.8

Health

Being healthy does not come about by chance.
Being healthy requires effort and balance,
both of which start with intentionality.

Introduction

Health is a subject that impacts many of the other life categories. If you are sick, not feeling well, or tired it can make other Life Goals almost impossible to achieve. It is extremely important that you maintain a balanced diet, get adequate sleep, and exercise. Staying fit will greatly increase your ability to achieve a better life.

Learn positive self-talk. Give yourself credit and rewards for successes and encourage yourself when the result is not what you wanted. Have a continual positive attitude regardless of the results.

Learn to take breaks, whether it is a twenty-minute power nap, five-minute walk each hour, or a two-week break from a big job.

Balance

Rest, relaxation, leisure, fun, exercise, and play, are all important parts of healthy living. The old saying, "All work and no play makes Jack a dull boy" is only partially true. We will not only be dull but we will also be tiresome, boring, and lacking the full enjoyment and experience of life.

Spending too much time doing any one thing, whether it is related to family, work, or pleasure, is not healthy. We should balance the activities in our lives and not ignore those things that make for healthy and happy living. We must take time to care for the spiritual, mental, emotional, and physical aspects of our lives.

We need balance in our lives!
There is a time for everything and everything has its time.

Manage Time Wisely

Time is one of our great personal resources. As human beings we have total control over how we use, invest, and spend our time. It is our very great responsibility to invest our time wisely. We can use it for something constructive or totally waste it. Unfortunately, time cannot be saved or accumulated for future use. It cannot be traded in on a better version and it cannot be replaced or recycled if it is wasted. We must, therefore, be diligent in how we use it.

Wise time management can bring
a healthy balance to our lives.

The challenge is to make the most of our time. Time is short, life is difficult, and many unplanned occurrences impact our schedules. However, we always seem to find the time to do the things we want to.

Here are some important questions to consider:

1. Do you eat meals with your family or with business associates?
2. What do you do with your extra time at lunch?
3. How much time do you spend around the coffee machine at work?
4. How much time do you spend schmoozing with friends?
5. Where do you spend your time at the end of the work day?
6. What do you talk about over dinner?
7. What do you do with your evenings?

8. How much time do you spend watching TV or playing videos games?
9. How late do you sleep on weekends?
10. Do you use your time wisely on weekends?

Don't Fret, Worry, or be Anxious

We should not be spending our time worrying about things that have no real significance in our lives. If we have no control over something it is useless to worry about it. We must free our minds from the debilitating effects of worry and anxiety. Worry has no positive impact on results.

Do not worry about people who succeed with their questionable schemes. You are not responsible or have anything to do with the success or failure of others. Who can produce a single positive result from fretting about some particular situation? Nothing is produced because of worry.

Let tomorrow worry about itself! Do not be concerned about things you cannot control. We can only control our actions, not the consequences.

Learn to be content in any circumstance.

Rest/Sleep

We need sleep. Going at full speed all the time will surely result in poor health, poor attitudes, and poor judgment. Why do many large corporations insist that their key management personnel take vacations? They need to relax, to get away, and forget about the daily stress in their jobs. They need to be refreshed.

Mothers of young children may need rest more than any other people we can identify. Dads, we challenge you to help your wives find the time they need to rest and be restored. Mothers have always had the sacred responsibility of raising children. But it is a real test of patience, stamina, and self-control to spend what must seem like every moment of your waking hours dealing with the needs of children.

Adequate rest is critical to your
physical, mental, and emotional health.

Relaxation

If you are in a stressful situation, you must find time to relax and take your mind off your circumstances. That usually means you have to do something else to distract yourself from the stress. The most important thing to do is get enough sleep. If you are tired in mind and body, your stress level will rise, and your efficiency will plummet.

Tips for relaxing:

1. Several times a day close your eyes for 2-3 minutes and think about restful things.

2. Make yourself relax during meals – eat slowly and talk about something other than work or your problems.

3. Certain activities can be restful to different people such as exercise (non-competitive), reading, listening to music, watching movies (TV, video, or film), taking a bath/shower, getting in a hot tub or sauna, having a massage, etc.

Pleasure

We must have a good understanding of the right priorities in life. We should spend our time wisely, because we have a limited time to make any impact on this earth. This means we must have a good balance between work and play.

Do you have a pleasure in your life that takes up too much of your time? How could you better use your time? We are not suggesting that you should give up all pleasures in favor of the ascetic life! What we do suggest is that you examine and evaluate your use of leisure time and recognize the importance of a balanced lifestyle.

PLANNING CATEGORY #8 – Health

Guidelines for drafting your Goal Statements:

1. They should be general and long-term in nature.
2. They should create some focus and direction for your life
3. They should indicate what you want to achieve in this area.
4. They might indicate what kind of person you want to be.

Examples of Possible Goal Statements

Planning: I will organize my time with daily "To-Do" lists.
Time: I will intentionally try to avoid wasting time.
Priorities: I will establish reasonable priorities in order to do the most important things first and on time.
Scheduling   I will organize and schedule my day.
Lifestyle: I will live a healthy lifestyle, giving adequate attention to both body and soul.
Balance: I will create the proper balance of time between work, family, and recreation.
Addiction: I will cease all addictive behavior.
Diet: I will follow a healthy diet. I will not regularly stock unhealthy things in the pantry.

Other goal statements might touch on such issues as healthy attitudes, healthy habits, rest and relaxation, worry, enjoyment of life, etc.

Draft Your Goal Statements

INSTRUCTION: Review the material above, and determine if any of these topics represent potential Life Goals for you. If so, write out the goals you may want to adopt below

Draft your own one or more goals for the category of HEALTH.

_____

_____

_____

_____

_____

_____

_____

_____

_____

_____

_____

_____

*"One of the most challenging aspects of our health journeys
is forgoing immediate pleasures for long-term rewards."*
Tammy Taylor[43]

*"Our greatest happiness does not depend on the condition of life in
which chance has placed us, but is always the result of a good
conscience, good health, occupation, and freedom in all just pursuits."*
Thomas Jefferson[44]

Chapter 8.9

Spiritual

"The two hardest tests on the spiritual road are the patience to wait for the right moment and the courage not to be disappointed with what we encounter."

Paulo Coelho[45]

General

We have left this category for last because the readers of this book could be of many faiths or none at all. We will not provide details about various faiths or beliefs, but we will give some generic information that anyone might use to develop a Spiritual Goal Statement. Given the process you have observed in previous chapters, you should be able to develop or create your own personal Spiritual Goal Statement. We will provide you some general guidance, but if you need more help, please contact your spiritual leaders or counselors.

Your task will be to draft a Goal Statement that is applicable to your own particular needs. Use the examples and the discussion provided to help you. If you are not a person of faith you can skip this chapter.

We have included a "Christian Perspective" in Appendix A. If you are a Christian, this might provide you with some different perspectives on preparing your Life Plan. Also be aware that we will publish a Christian Wisdom Series after the Life Planning Series is published. This will provide some different and additional perspectives for the Christian who has purchased one of the books in the Life Planning Series.

Comparative Religious Doctrines

NOTE: We have chosen to illustrate information about five of the major religions. The basic question that must be answered is not the nature of the belief, but whether it is _true._

Christian	Jew	Islam	Mormon	Jehovah Witness
Founder:				
Jesus Christ 30 AD	Abraham/Moses 2000 BC	Muhammad 570 AD	Joseph Smith 1830 AD	Charles Russell 1879
Who is God?				
Monotheistic: One true God, but with 3 natures Jesus = God Jesus = Messiah Bible = Truth	Monotheistic: Only one God and one person Jesus = false prophet (not Messiah)	Monotheistic: Only one God and one person Jesus=sinless prophet SON = blasphemy	(1) Eternal Father (2) Omnipresent-no (3) No Trinity Jesus = pre-existent spirit and a brother to man	(1) One Jehovah (2) No Trinity (3) Holy Spirit is force, not person Jesus = man Jesus not God
Man's Destiny - Where is man headed?				
Spend eternity with God in heaven: --personal existence --fellowship w God Or, eternal hell	Various: --nothing after death --be with Messiah	Join Allah in heaven for eternity of sensual pleasure and gratification	Heaven	(1) Eternal Life (2) Eternal Hell does not exist 144,000->heaven Others-->earth
Problem:				
(1) Rebellion (2) Sin (3) Separation from God	(1) Impurity (2) Alienation from God	(1) Disobedience, but atonement not needed	(1) Adam right in sinning, but (2) Punish man for sin	All born to sin, because Adam sinned
How Does Man Achieve His Destiny?				
(1) Accept Jesus as Savior as payt. for sin-debt (2) Based on faith, not works of man	(1) Repent - moral life (2) Observe Law (3) No assurance	(1) Submission (2) Earn it: (a) believe in 5 doctrines (b) perform duties of 5 Pillars of Faith (c) depends on behavior - not sure	(1) Obedience to laws of Bible (2) Baptism is necessary gateway to heaven	By faith + good works Must prove worthiness

> ## *IMPORTANT:*
> Everyone has his or her own spiritual journey. It will not be the same experience for everyone. Your degree of knowledge, understanding, and wisdom related to spiritual things will occur at a time and place that is unique to you. But you can either hinder or help in the revelation of truth. If you have closed your heart and mind to finding your spiritual home, you may struggle with finding truth. Be intentional on finding your spiritual future and learning the truth.

Behavior and Habits

Look over the behavior listed below and circle those that are a particular problem for you. If you don't find your "favorites" anywhere on the list, write them on the blank lines at the bottom.

Blasphemy	Boastfulness	Persecution	Corruption
Covetousness	Deceitfulness	Injustice	Selfishness
Lying	Foolishness	Ignoring God	Pride
Rebellion	Disobedience	Fraud	Hypocrisy
Hatred	Anger	Perversity	Destructiveness
Envy	Impudence	Lust	Unruliness
Ingratitude	Hostility to God	Unholiness	Ungodliness
Prayerlessness	Mischievousness	_____	_____
_____	_____		

Spiritual Subjects

The following subjects may help you get started. They are not intended to be all-inclusive. You need to decide what applies to your life situation. Circle any particular subjects you feel apply to you.

Sin	Obedience	Holy and Righteous Living
Forgiveness	Repentance	Education/Spiritual Growth
Discipleship	Heaven/Hell	Prayer/Meditation
Worship	Stewardship	Lifestyle
Faithfulness	Faith/belief	Restoration
Life Change	Miracles	Community/Fellowship

Spiritual Questions

You may be in a situation where you have never been introduced to God or religion of any kind. You may be a seeker with many questions. You may question whether God really exists. If you are a member of a particular religion, we will assume you have the ability to develop any necessary and appropriate Life Goals relative to your religion.

If you are a seeker and trying to determine the truth about the divine, we encourage you to aggressively seek the truth.

There are two other categories of people. One is the atheist who does not believe in the existence of a God or any gods. The other is the agnostic who believes that one cannot determine the existence of God one way or the other. The agnostic believes God cannot be known and is therefore unwilling to commit to an opinion about the existence of God.

If you are either an atheist or agnostic you have every right to those beliefs. We would have you consider the following: If you are right that God does not exist or cannot be determined, and you are correct in those beliefs, then there will never be any consequences because of your beliefs. But if you are wrong, the consequences are significant – it's a matter of life and death.

Therefore, we suggest that you confirm without any doubt your position on the existence of God. We believe that many people adopt one of these two positions in order not to face a decision about God. If you are one of those people, you need to prove or confirm your beliefs.

How sure are you that you are right?

If you believe that God probably does exist, but you don't know what to believe, here are some questions you might want to think about:

1. Do you believe in life after death?
2. If you believe in life after death, how is that achieved?
3. Do you believe in heaven and hell?
4. If you believe in heaven or hell, what determines where you will go?
5. Do you believe in moral absolutes?

6. Do you believe in absolute truth and the inherent existence of right and wrong?
7. Who determines what is right and wrong?
8. Assuming there is a god, can you live a life acceptable to that god? Can you live a sinless life?
9. Given that you sin (rebellion against a god) then how do you prevent punishment for the sins you commit? Or, how do you receive forgiveness for those sins?
10. Do you have reason to believe any of the world's religions? Why? Why not?
11. Do any of the religions explain why the innocent suffer?
12. Do you know anyone that has been transformed by their religion?

PLANNING CATEGORY #9 – Spiritual

Guidelines for drafting your Goal Statements:

1. They should be general and long-term in nature.
2. They should create some focus and direction for your life
3. They should indicate what you want to achieve in this area.
4. They might indicate what kind of person you want to be.

Examples of Possible Goal Statements:

Truth: I will determine whether or not God exists.
Seeking: I will intentionally seek out the truth and determine what I should believe.
Sin: I will determine how my sin can be forgiven and how I can be right with God.
Eternal Life: I will determine the requirements for gaining eternal life.

Draft Your Goal Statements

INSTRUCTION: Review the material above, and determine if any of these topics represent potential Life Goals for you. If so, write out the goals you may want to adopt below:

Draft your own one or more goals for the category of SPIRITUAL.

_____

_____

_____

_____

_____

_____

_____

_____

_____

_____

_____

_____

_____

"It is easy enough to be friendly to one's friends.
But to befriend the one who regards himself as your enemy
is the quintessence of true religion. The other is mere business."
Mahatma Gandhi[46]

"Remember that the fool in the eyes of the gods
and the fool in the eyes of man are very different."
Oscar Wilde[47]

Chapter 9

PERSONAL MISSION STATEMENT – FINAL

"My mission in life is not merely to survive,
but to thrive; and to do so with some passion,
some compassion, some humor, and some style."
Maya Angelou[48]

General

You have made great progress and we are nearing the point at which you can begin thinking about what you are actually going to do to accomplish your Goals. We simply need to review, finalize and pull the process together. The first step will be to finalize your Personal Mission Statement. However, before you proceed, we would like to comment on the quote above.

Angelou has clearly indicated that she does not want to live a boring existence. She wants to do life in style and with a passion. She is telling herself that she is going to be intentional about her life and not allow the vagaries of life to dictate her lifestyle. In addition she indicates she wants to live her life with humor and compassion.

Angelou can now measure all her opportunities or challenges against this standard to determine if she wants to participate or not. If she does decide to do something, she is going to do it in style with a dash of compassion, and with a bit of humor. There is nothing more impressive than someone who can laugh at him or herself.

Stop and think for a moment if this were your life mission statement. Would it give you real practical guidance if you were trying to make a significant decision in your life? We think so!

Review

In Chapter 5 you developed your <u>preliminary</u> Personal Mission Statement. We will now finalize that work.

Since the completion of the preliminary draft in Chapter 5 you have identified your Life Priorities, Commitments, and Goals. It is possible that along the way you made some revisions to your initial draft in Chapter 5.

Before you copy the latest version into this chapter, take some time to review your priorities, commitments, and goals and make any changes to your preliminary Personal Mission Statement that would reflect your current life thinking and perspectives.

Ask yourself if you have developed anything in these areas that would cause you to modify your life mission or purpose. Make the necessary changes to your Mission Statement in Chapter 5.

Updated Personal Mission Statement

After any and all changes, copy your latest version of your Mission Statement in the space below:

_____

_____

_____

_____

_____

_____

_____

_____

_____

_____

Re-evaluation and Review

You have now spent considerable time examining your life and goals relative to a number of life categories. It is possible that this process has raised some questions in your mind relative to your Personal Mission Statement. You may have found or sense that the basic vision for your life is different than you first thought. We want you to re-evaluate your Personal Mission Statement in light of your present thinking and particularly in regard to the goals and objectives you have developed for your life.

Let's review again what we are doing and what we want your Personal Mission Statement to say. We have defined a **Personal Mission Statement** to be a broad general statement aimed at identifying your primary purpose in life. It is the rationale or justification for your existence. It may indicate the activities you intend to perform, the kind of person you want to be, or major goals you want to accomplish. It says what you want your life to be all about. It may include the following:

- reason you exist,
- activities or functions you want to perform,
- the kind of person you wish to be, or
- a vision of what you want to become or seek to do in life.

In general, we might expect your Personal Mission Statement to address one or more of the following:

- your spiritual goals;
- your character;
- what type of steward you want to be with your time, talents, skills, and resources;
- your attitude toward your family relationships or friends;
- how you will use your money and wealth;
- what type of spouse and/or parent you want to be;

Review and Modification

You have already made adjustments for your priorities, commitments, and goals. Now consider some of the concepts mentioned above. Your

Personal Mission Statement describes the area of time and space where you will impact the world. It should also describe the nature of what you will do in that space. Does your current draft do that for you?

Closely review your current Personal Mission Statement and determine if it accurately reflects the focus and direction you want in your life. Does it say what is right for you? Does it describe what you want to do or accomplish? Look again at the questions and issues outlined above. Are you satisfied? If not, re-write your Personal Mission Statement.

Examples of Personal Mission Statements

These examples may or may not address some of the applicable areas of your life. Use these ideas and concepts as guidelines in finalizing your own Personal Mission Statement.

1. To live my life based on the highest moral and ethical standards, living a life of balance and moderation.

2. To be honest, live with integrity, and base my life on truth, exhibiting a caring and gentle attitude to my family, fellow workers, and business associates.

3. To be hard-working and diligent in my career as well as trustworthy, dependable, and reliable.

4. To be a good steward of my time, talents, and financial resources, serving others through helping the needy and disadvantaged in my community.

5. To be the very best parent (mother/father) that I can possibly be, raising my children in a loving atmosphere and teaching them to make a constructive contribution to society.

6. To be a student of understanding and wisdom, seeking knowledge by reading, studying, and teaching, in order to convey the truth to others.

7. To use my financial success to help the disadvantaged and needy by annually giving a significant contribution to various people

and charities who assist the needy, care for the sick, and tend to the poor.

8.   To have a vibrant, personal, growing relationship with God by optimizing the use of my God-given talents, resources, and spiritual gifts to help others grow in their faith.

These examples were written after much personal thought – they're **not** first drafts, so don't let them intimidate you! Alternatively, you could have a very simple Personal Mission Statement: *"I will be honest in all I do and say."* Make your mission statement work for you.

Final Personal Mission Statement:

_____
_____
_____
_____
_____
_____
_____
_____
_____
_____
_____
_____
_____
_____
_____

"Our prime purpose in this life is to help others.
And if you can't help them, at least don't hurt them."
Dalai Lama[49]

"The purpose of life is not to be happy. It is to be useful, to be
honorable, to be compassionate, to have it make some difference
that you have lived and lived well."
Ralph Waldo Emerson[50]

Chapter 10

Review – Adjust – Update
and
Make Changes

*"Life is a series of natural and spontaneous changes.
Don't resist them – that only creates sorrow. Let reality be reality.
Let things flow naturally forward in whatever way they like."*
Lao Tzu[51]

*"If you don't like something change it; if you can't change it,
change the way you think about it."*
Mary Engelbreit[52]

Let's stop, review and make changes. This would be a good time before you finalize your plan to do a quick but thorough review to ensure that all you have done is consistent. If it is not, make the changes necessary so that all phases and subjects are in harmony.

You may have identified a goal that is not consistent with your priorities. You may need to add something to your priorities and commitments because of your goals or your final mission statement. So review the following subjects and make sure everything works together and there are no inconsistences.

- Core Values – Chapter 4
- Life Priorities – Chapter 6
- Life Commitments – Chapter 7
- Life Goals – Chapter 8
- Personal Mission Statement (final) – Chapter 9

Make any necessary changes and proceed to finalizing your Goals in the next chapter.

"There are two kinds of fools:
those who can't change their opinions
and those who won't."
Josh Billings[53]

Chapter 11

Life Goals - Final

"Our greatest happiness does not depend on the condition of life in which chance has placed us, but is always the result of a good conscience, good health, occupation, and freedom in all just pursuits."
Thomas Jefferson[54]

Life Goals from Chapter 8

INSTRUCTION: Enter the latest version of your Life Goals you identified in Chapter 8. Enter the final version after any changes or revisions. You will do a final review and make any necessary adjustments later in this chapter. If you have multiple goals in any particular category enter them as well. We have provided excess space, if needed.

Miscellaneous examples:

MAKING GOOD CHOICES
I will learn how to make good decisions.

BEING INTENTIONAL
I will think and consider my choices before I take action.
I will take positive action based on my goals and objectives.

CONTROLLING THE SENSES

I will filter and control what I think, see, hear, and touch because they influence my decisions.

PLANNING

I will chart a PATH, have a PLAN, and know where I am going.

Goals – #1 Life Principles

_____
_____
_____
_____
_____
_____
_____
_____

Goals – #2 Habits

_____
_____
_____
_____
_____
_____
_____
_____

Goals – #3 Relationships

_____
_____
_____
_____
_____
_____
_____
_____

Goals – # 4 Work

_____
_____
_____
_____
_____
_____
_____
_____
_____

Goals – #5 Education

_____
_____
_____
_____
_____
_____
_____
_____
_____

Goals – #6 Community Service

_____
_____
_____
_____
_____
_____
_____
_____

Goals – #7 Wealth and Finances

_____
_____
_____
_____
_____
_____
_____
_____
_____

Goals – #8 Health

_____
_____
_____
_____
_____
_____
_____
_____
_____

Goals - #9 Spiritual

_____
_____
_____
_____
_____
_____
_____
_____
_____

Review

1. Do you need to add or delete anything from your goals above? Add or delete them.

2. Do you need to combine any similar goals? Combine them.

3. Do you need to modify or delete any goal based on your _Final_ Personal Mission Statement? Do you need to add anything in order to accomplish your Mission?

Goal Priorities

It would be wonderful to think that you could work on the entire Life Plan and accomplish all these goals in the next several months. That's not realistic! You may be able to accomplish some of them immediately, but others may have a time-frame of years. Focus on what is most important and reduce your initial undertaking to a manageable level. Prioritize all the Goals into one of the following categories by entering the following priority codes next to each goal.

"I"	Immediate:	must be addressed as soon as possible
"H"	High:	work on these during the next six months
"M"	Medium:	work on some of these in the next year, but these are not critical
"L"	Low:	can wait until the more important plans are under way or completed

Start Dates

To the right of <u>each</u> goal that you have prioritized as "I" or "H" indicate the date you want to begin working on that particular issue. End dates at this point are probably unrealistic.

Caution

There are two problems you may encounter in respect to "Plans." The first is that you begin to see the plans as "set in concrete," making it difficult for you to change direction. It is, therefore, absolutely imperative that you think of your Life Plan as a _working document_ that can be changed at any time. Secondly, once your Life Plan is written, you may find it easy to put it away and never review or discuss it again. It is critical to work on the actions steps if you want to make some changes in your life. It is also important to review, update, and amend the plan as conditions and circumstances in your life change.

Establish a regular time to review your progress. Once a month, quarter, or every six months, sit down and review where you are. What have you accomplished? Do you need to revise your priorities? Do you need help? What is not working? What is working? What changes do you need to make to your plan?

Chapter 12

IMPLEMENTATION: How To Do It

"Life can be simple and beautiful.
Focus on the good things."
Maxime Lagacé[55]

Part A – Impacting My Heart

Filter and control what you think, see, hear, and touch because
they will influence your heart, which in turn influences your decisions.

The Senses

Our senses are the gateway to gaining knowledge, understanding, and ultimately wisdom. Such information can be both positive and negative depending on the source of the information we are receiving. For example, if all we ever listen to is classical music we will ultimately become very knowledgeable about the writers and performers and we may even choose to learn to play an instrument because we love the music. The music has touched our heart and we not only want to listen, but to participate.

If we live in a home where one or more of the parents are abusive, that abusive behavior becomes the natural order of life. We grow up in an environment where abuse (physical, mental, and emotional) is the norm and we mimic such behavior in our own lives.

The nature of our surroundings, what we hear – see – touch, will have great influence on our thinking and behaviors. If we are constantly listening to music that is vulgar, violent, or sexually explicit, that message creeps, if not stampedes, into our hearts and becomes acceptable because our minds and hearts have been conditioned to live out what our senses experience.

Consider the young boy or girl who is a tennis pro at age 16. How did they become so good at playing tennis? Aside from the fact that they may have some natural physical talent, the one thing that these gifted athletes have in common is they spent hours and hours on the tennis court – every day. They ate, drank, and slept tennis. Tiger Woods didn't become a great golfer because he had a natural swing. He is a great golfer because his dad had him playing golf every waking minute.

I say all this to help you understand that what you experience (think, see, hear, touch) will have a great influence on your life. That influence could be life-changing if you spend enough time in any given activity. What we are doing and what our senses are experiencing will influence our lives and that influence can be good and bad. When that influence reaches the heart and saturates our inner being we have established or created a core value that will dictate actions and decisions. Thus, it is fundamentally important to arrange your life so that your experience influences your heart in the right manner.

The Heart

Each of us has an inner place where our true self exists and that place is the ultimate source for our decisions. It represents who we truly are. For the purposes of this book we are choosing to describe that place as the "heart."

The heart is the seat of our emotions, understanding, reason, conscience, motives, desires, decision-making, and faith. The heart represents who I am or my real self (the inner me). It is the central core of my being because it influences all the important choices in my life and represents the true me.

Thus, the heart defines or determines who you are, both good and bad. The heart is the ultimate source for making every important decision. All key decisions or actions will ultimately come from the heart.

I do not mean to imply that we make decisions based on emotions, although that can happen on occasion. Rather, we process knowledge and information through our mind and other senses, evaluate that information against our core values, and arrived at conclusions that represent our position or belief about that particular subject.

If I am going to shape my life and my character I must impact or change my heart because it is the place in my inner being where I make the most important life decisions.

The Mind

In order for something to be written on the heart it must to be filtered through the mind. I must go through the process of convincing my intellect that something is true or desirable so that my heart will allow me to act on that concept, information, or principle. It will not be enough to say I believe something to be true. I must have accepted that truth and be committed to implementing it in my life.

You may want to pause in your reading and think about this concept for a minute.

1. What are your eyes and ears seeing and hearing these days? What are they used to absorbing?

2. What or who are you listening to that is influencing your life?

3. What are you seeing that is implanting impressions on your mind and ultimately your heart?

4. What are you touching (where are you going) that is establishing your value system?

5. How are all these inputs to your heart and mind influencing your behavior?

We might like to think that a little harmless seeing and listening won't really have any impact, but that has proven not to be the case.

The heart ultimately determines our decisions and direction. But the mind is a powerful filter that impacts what our hearts will consider. If we want to change some fundamental characteristics in our life, we will need new information and understanding to reach the heart. But our minds must allow us to do that. If we want to change our hearts we need to condition our minds to prepare our hearts for new input. It will be difficult to change our lives if our minds remain rigid and stubborn.

We need to stretch or open our minds to new thoughts and new ideas as well as close them to evil or useless information. What we think about will ultimately be who or what we are. If our thoughts are constantly about money and wealth our actions will soon reflect those thoughts because our hearts have been saturated with thoughts about riches, expensive cars, or big houses.

On the other hand, if we want to change our lifestyle and we begin filling our minds with information and knowledge about positive behavior, the heart will receive the message and change, even transforming change. But that change will not likely occur unless the input from our senses is filtered in the mind and appropriately impacts the heart producing a revised set of standards or desires.

Thus, we are back to the need to be _intentional_. I must decide I want to change and then be intentional about filling the pipeline to my heart with information and knowledge that will transform my heart such that I can easily make the right choices. That will happen when my heart has been conditioned to produce the results I desire.

> *"She knew the power of her mind and*
> *so programmed it for success."*
> Carrie Green[56]

Solomon's Wisdom

King Solomon of the Bible was a wealthy and powerful ruler of Israel. Most people, if asked what King Solomon was known for, would answer, "wisdom," remembering that he asked God for wisdom and God granted that request. It's true that Solomon is remembered for his great wisdom, but what he actually asked God for was not wisdom, but a discerning heart in order to do two things; (1) govern his people, and (2) to distinguish between right and wrong. Both of these are dependent on having a discerning heart.[57]

The heart (and its nature) is a critical concept in our understanding if we desire to direct, change, and transform our actions and behavior. The inner self must accept and decide (discern) to filter the barrage of sensory information that blasts us from every angle.

We must keep our hearts and minds on the right path.

The Power of Thought

I can remember my Dad saying to me on several occasions, "God gave you a brain. Use it!" Thinking seems to be a lost art these days! Many problems would disappear if we would take time to think. Not every answer has to be determined in 10 seconds.

If you are being challenged with an important issue or question, you need to produce the right answer. Thinking about important issues and questions is what successful people do. I have a motto I live by in these situations. If you insist on my answer right now, the answer is, "No."

There are few things that can't wait at least 24 hours. I was gifted with a somewhat suspicious nature, so if you approach me with some new idea, or some fantastic opportunity, my response is likely to be, "Prove it." That pause often saves me from making mistakes. Thinking a problem through in order to understand all the ramifications will lead to better solutions.

Other people do not necessarily have our best interests in mind. They have their own agenda and are often looking for companions to accompany them. Unfortunately the reason they want company is because it will validate their own poor judgment. Even friends can lead us down a path we don't want to travel if we are not diligent.

Since my thoughts are dramatically impacted by what I see, what I hear, and where I go, I need to determine my decisions to see, hear, and go based on my own core values, goals, and standards. I remember reading the question, "If all you ever listened to for ten years was country music, what would you believe?" I wasn't really sure what the author was getting at until I read his answer:

a. Everyone drinks beer and is rowdy on Saturday night.

b. Everyone owns a dog who is their best friend.

c. Everyone owns a pick-up truck.

d. Everyone's girl leaves!

That's funny, right? Well, it may be funny but it's also true. We become what we do. We establish values and opinions based on what we hear, see, and touch. All the techies in the reading audience have been waiting to read their favorite computer example: GIGO (Garbage In – Garbage Out). And, it's true. If you put information in your computer that is wrong, misleading, or ill-advised, (garbage), then that's what will come out as answers to your questions. The computer can only produce answers based on what it has been fed.

We are the same way. If we feed our minds and hearts garbage, then that's what we are going to get back. A lifestyle based on garbage is not very attractive.

Fix Your Mind on What is True

Fix your mind on what is good, true, and wholesome. A changed heart can transform your life, but only if it is not fed garbage. So, give thought to what you are doing! Focus your attention on things that are healthy and true, on subjects that uplift and do not tear down.

The fool will believe anything. He does not give thought to his ways.

"Giving thought to our ways" seems like a simple solution. But that simple truth is dependent on taking action that the thought produces. Be intentional! If we give thought to our ways we can determine the best course of action, particularly if we have taken some time to think about it. My first question in any situation where a significant decision must be made is, "What are the alternatives?" If you don't consider any alternatives and their likely impact, your first thoughts generally seem right. Decisions made in haste often fail miserably when compared with other possible alternatives.

If you are faced with a question you have already thought about, you probably have several possible answers already in mind. Why? You know already how you want to respond because you have previously thought about it.

For example, I have already thought through the question of whether I am going to give a female co-worker a ride home alone because she is stranded. It doesn't really make any difference that I will be going right by her apartment. I'll put her in a cab and send her home – I'm not going to violate one of my core values. I can produce that response because I have thought about the situation in advance.

Think about the challenges to your core values. Think about the possible temptations that would cause you to violate your values. What will you do when these challenges and temptations occur? If you have already considered these challenges and thought about your response, the answers are easy. That's why core values are valuable. They require you to think in advance about what is important to you.

For example, if you choose honesty, integrity, and truth, your life becomes much simpler when you are faced with issues or requests that tempt you to do things that would violate those values.

> *"Your mind is precious. It has the power to*
> *unlock infinite possibilities."*
> Joel Annesley[58]

FOUR KEY DECISIONS

How are you going to harness your heart and mind to produce the results you desire? What must you do? What are the practical actions you can take to control what you see? How do you establish limits on what you hear? What should you avoid?

First you must want to make improvements in your life. Then, you must intentionally take action that will either limit your exposure to negative input or open up the possibilities for new, improved, and positive experiences that will begin transforming your heart.

REALITY CHECK! You may be thinking that it sounds like a lot of work and effort to make these changes in your life. That may be true! It really depends on your starting point. If you are struggling with the need to change bad behavior or bad habits it may take real time and effort. But what is the alternative?

Successful people have been practicing these activities for many years and it may be second nature to them. If you struggle with some of the Life Commitments you have identified, it will require some effort. The first step is this: Just get started.

Decision #1: I will filter what I see.

First, take one step at a time. Most of us are not prepared to make many drastic changes all at once. So how do we get started? Ask yourself where the negative input is coming from? What are you reading? What are you watching on TV, the Internet, or your phone? Tackle your big and most serious bad habit first. Do it with a passion.

If your problem is the TV, turn it off. If you can't do that, cancel the service. That may sound drastic, but it may be that a drastic action is needed!

You will be amazed how quickly you can adapt to a TV-free environment. If the political noise between the Republicans and Democrats is causing you to be angry all the time, stop watching the talking heads who are only performing so that you will watch and see the commercials. Have you ever thought about that? News is no longer news. News has become a channel to change your way of thinking.

What are you reading? If you are reading trash, your mind is full of trash and just like our oceans it will eventually cough up all the discarded trash onto the beach. If that beach is in your boss' office, the results may not be what you desire.

The secret of success is to focus on what you want to change or transform. Put limitations on certain activities and focus your attention on what you want to change. Choose one activity at a time and face it down until it is under control and then go to the next. Once you are successful with getting one questionable activity under control, it is much easier to tackle the next.

You can change and make new habits
by practicing them for 30 days.

Filter what you see!

Decision #2: I will filter what I hear.

Who or what are you listening to? I stopped listening to talk shows that want to get me all excited about some topic. I realized some time ago it wasn't good for my mental health. I also realized I couldn't trust the truthfulness of what was being said. Everything seemed to be slanted to influence me toward some position that they, the programmers, wanted to promote.

So, I stopped. After a short time I didn't miss it at all because I found other things I wanted to hear, read, or visit. TV, radio, and podcasts can either encourage or poison our minds. They can bring calm or cause stress and anxiousness. They can drive you crazy and take over your mind. But if you choose what you hear with forethought, the listening can be uplifting, educational, and soothing.

The music we listen to will often influence us more than we think. Young people are particularly impacted by music. Have you ever listened to the actual words of some of the edgy music these days? People who think they have to speak in vulgarities, sexually explicit language, or other shocking ways are not the people I want to listen to or people I want my children to hear.

These people are not simply expressing their free thought and right to speak openly, they are damaging everyone who listens. Sadly, they don't really care. They want attention and shocking, explicit language is their hook.

That hook pierces my veil of decency, so I reject their attempt to poison my mind and heart. You must do the same. Our goal must be to control and filter the voices of evil, discord, and rebellion in order to feed our hearts information that is uplifting and positive.

So if you are among those who need help in this area of your life, consider yourself challenged. If this is not a particularly problem for you, feel blessed. You may have a friend who needs your advice in this area of their life.

Filter what you hear!

Decision #3: I will filter where I go.

I will avoid places that cause me difficulty or create negative temptations. If I am married, I will never be alone with a person of the opposite sex who is not my spouse. If I am an alcoholic, I will not go to bars. If I have a gambling problem, I will not go to the casinos. If I have an addiction problem, I will not hang out where that addiction can be fed. If I have an eating problem, I will not go to "all you can eat" establishments. It's not that difficult to draw the line.

The problem is in choosing to cross or not to cross that line. It is very easy to identify those places that will cause us temptation. I simply make the decision to avoid those places.

On the positive side I *will* go to places that will encourage me, support me, and give me peace. I need to go places where I will grow spiritually, intellectually, and emotionally. I need to go where the activity produces joy and satisfaction, not temptation, worry, and stress.

One of the biggest temptations may be with our friends who have other agendas. Don't be persuaded to get off your path by friends or acquaintances who don't really understand your mindset. Sometimes it might be necessary to give up old friends and make new ones.

Filter where you go!

Decision 4: I will filter what I say.

Many of us are very careless about our speech and the impact it has on other people. Some even think that they can say anything they wish simply because it is their right.

Gracious speech is polite and shows respect to the one we are talking to. It is pleasing and acceptable, not grating, harsh, or vulgar. It has some lasting value and is appropriate for the situation.

The one who speaks too quickly or speaks without thinking is worse than a fool. This is a serious warning to those who speak up and then think later. Speaking quickly means that our words may have little thought behind them. The result can be embarrassing and in retrospect should have been left unsaid.

Thinking before you speak can be a lifesaver. Obviously you want to have something worthwhile to contribute and pausing before you speak can often produce a good result. You don't want to say something hurtful or off-putting. Your comments should be helpful, useful, and on target.

It is always wise to consider if what you are saying is adding to the conversation, or just meaningless comments. Have you listened long enough that you understand the discussion? Is what you want to say actually worth saying? Is it just repeating or rehashing what someone else has said?

Under no circumstance should you lie, embellish, or shade what you are saying. Do not slander. Words can have gigantic negative impact. With technology today your words can go around the world in seconds and impact people you don't know and will never meet. Your words can start fires or put them out.

Choose your words carefully.

DISCIPLINE

The key to being intentional is *discipline*. It is like the cross-country runner or marathoner who is training to run a race. He or she needs to be disciplined enough to practice running. Their sessions aren't just once in a while. They,re every day! The runner needs to build up stamina and muscle tone. He needs to make his body know what to expect and be ready to run the race, hit the exhaustion wall, and continue running. Control is gained by enforcing obedience to an order or regimen. The runner wants to have an orderly or prescribed response when times get tough during the race. Self-control is mandatory.

This is true for us as well. We need to be disciplined about where we go, what we see, and what we hear. We need to be sharp mentally and emotionally. We must make daily decisions that will put us in the right places so that what we see, what we hear, and where we go will have positives influences on our character.

If this is particularly difficult for you, find a trusted friend or family member to hold you accountable. Give them friend permission to challenge you as well as encourage you. Agree you will not lie about your activities.

My heart will be impacted by
what I see, what I hear, and where I go!

Part B – Being Intentional

General

If you are not sure how committed you want to be, these quotes might encourage you:

"Many of life's failures are people who did not realize how close they were to success when they gave up."
Thomas A. Edison[59]

"Each life is made up of mistakes and learning, waiting and growing, practicing patience and being persistent."
Billy Graham[60]

*"Life isn't about finding yourself.
Life is about creating yourself."*
George Bernard Shaw[61]

"The quality of a person's life is in direct proportion to their commitment to excellence, regardless of their chosen field of endeavor."
Vince Lombardi[62]

This fact remains: You are the one that must decide that you want to be the very best you can be. There is really not much we can suggest unless you really want to live a better life. If you walk away and just "want to" without any "going to" the result will be just like the results of the slacker – *nada*. This is where the commitment to diligence and hard work has real meaning in your life. This is where you decide and commit!

We will give you some tips on being intentional in the rest of this section, but if you don't claim possession of it, you won't get it. Make a decision right now that nothing is going to dissuade you from your goal to live a better life.

What is the plan for the rest of the book?

1. In the rest of this chapter we will discuss how to live an *intentional life*.

2. The next chapter will teach you how to develop your Action Steps for your Life Plan.

3. After the Actions Steps we will discuss living a life of hope, satisfaction, and contentment.

4. Finally, we will outline the coaching services we can provide to help you complete your plan and/or implement your Actions Steps.

5. Additional help is provided at the end of the book in four Appendices:

> Appendix A – Christian Perspective
> Appendix B – How to Prioritize
> Appendix C – How to Schedule (time management)
> Appendix D – Decision-making

Being Intentional

Being intentional means making choices and decisions and carrying them out. It means committing to some course of action and following through. Being intentional does not mean that all the right choices are made, but failures or mistakes are left on the field of play. The committed person does not fail because he was not in the game!

You cannot succeed unless you actively and intentionally decide to be engaged. A fulfilled life does not happen if all you do is think and read about it. It happens because you make thoughtful choices aimed at being the best you can be, and then you do it.

The opposite of being intentional is being unplanned or inadvertent. It results in drifting, like buffaloes on a range wandering from one patch of grass to another without any thought of where they are going. If we are not intentional we will just wander through life trying to avoid the potholes. Spending our lives climbing out of potholes is not an attractive lifestyle.

Why be Intentional?

I want all life has to give me and I want to be able to say when it's over that I did my best. I'm not interested in just surviving. I want to live with the expectation that life will reward me if and when I make the effort to make it the best it can be.

I want to be admired by others because I set the right example and I did the right thing. I want family and friends to know I care enough about life and about them that I will make sacrifices for them. I want to be honest and demonstrate to others that life can be good if you want it to be. Yes, bad things happen to good people, but that is the exception, not the rule.

I want to live my life knowing that making good decisions and commitments will dramatically impact the quality of my life. I will not make myself the victim by allowing life to just happen to me; I will make decisions and choices that will shape my life.

What do <u>YOU</u> want out of life? You can begin a dramatic transformation in your life when you decide to be intentional and just do it!

I will intentionally take action to make changes in my life!

Making it Happen!

A good life, success, and happiness don't just happen. You cannot fix the results of bad choices simply by being sorry you made them. The good life starts with making good decisions, making commitments, and fixing mistakes. Being intentional!

The easy part here is making the decision to do something. The harder part is carrying out the decisions you make to live a better life. But the real test comes when those decisions result in difficulties and problems. Are you going to turn tail and run at the first sight of trouble? Be prepared for difficulties and realize that the only answer is to persevere. Don't let fear, confusion, or setbacks dissuade you from your pursuit.

Tips for being Intentional

AUTOPILOT:
What percentage of your life is on autopilot? This is where I found myself in 2018 and early in 2019. I was going through a part of my life without thinking and I had lost touch with some of the important major goals in my life.

Therefore my actions, responses, and activities were being done without much thought and very little, if any, passion. I had to get away and spend some quiet time, pray, meditate, and give some serious thought to my life. What had happened? How had I gotten off track? What did I want and what did I not want out of life?

I got my life off auto pilot by becoming intentional about activities that I had allowed to become routine. I was doing them without thinking, caring, or being engaged. I focused on the problem, made some new choices, and began the process of change. I set some new goals in order to drive myself out of the rut. And it worked. It always works when you make a good decision and then follow through.

GOALS:
The reason it worked for me was that I knew what I wanted and I knew where I wanted to be. I just needed to be intentional about getting there. Do you know where you want to be? Have you established any life goals that are guiding your daily routines? Have you made bad choices in the past because you did not have a clear idea of where you were going?

Outstanding people and effective leaders all have goals, whether stated or unstated. They know what they want and they determine a path that will help them achieve their objectives. They develop skills and habits that will propel them along so that regardless of where they are in their journey, they know the goal.

POWER TO SUCCEED

1. Adopt the motto, "I can do this."

2. Accept and take responsibility for your decisions. If you make a mistake, correct it and move on. Mistakes and poor choices will happen. Fix them and learn from them.

3. Reject the concept that, "This is just the way things are."

4. Adopt actions that will enhance your chance for success:

> a. Take control of your life and your calendar. You are not too busy to succeed!
>
> b. Have a plan and work it.
>
> c. Take control of your health. Eat right. Get adequate sleep and exercise.
>
> d. Be positive. Abandon all the negative self-talk.
>
> e. Simplify your life, if necessary. You will be amazed by the impact of a simple life!

5. Remember that this will take time. Don't be in a big rush.

6. Be focused. Make your yes a YES, and your no a NO. You can't do everything.

7. Take action. Make the necessary decisions. Be in control of your life. Don't allow life to simply happen to you. Nothing will happen until you do something.

Remember:

> a. You are not entitled.
> b. You are not perfect.
> c. Action requires your energy and your commitment.
> d. Habits are formed by believing in yourself and repeating the desired activity until it becomes your natural response.

FIRM FOUNDATION

1. Acquire knowledge in order to generate understanding that will ultimately produce wisdom.
2. Recognize that you will make many decisions and every decision has a consequence.

3. Decide you are going to do it. Commit to persevering.
4. Know the landscape! Where is your life? What is impacting your life today? What is working and what is not working? What do you need to change?
5. Are you fearful? What are those fears? Address the fears you have. Are the fears valid?
6. Do you really know your strengths and weaknesses?

Finally, keep your eye on the goal. Know what you want to achieve. Seek a better life. Don't allow others to determine your present or your future. Establish your own standards and values. Know what you want. Harmony, peace, and rest are possible if you want them – but you must want them. You must want to live a better life and to improve your circumstances.

Decide, and then do it!
If you are not intentional – nothing happens!

Be Flexible

One of the biggest hurdles in making life changes is finding time. You're too busy. I'm too busy. We are all too busy! Thus, managing our time is an important part of being intentional.

How are you spending your time? Are you exhausted at the end of the day? Do you even have time to think about being intentional? I am sure you have heard, "Time is our most valuable asset." It can be! Remember, you cannot recycle time. Once time is gone, you can't get it back.

New issues and problems will enter our lives at the most inopportune times. Joy can occur at the most unexpected times. Be prepared to be unprepared. Be flexible! Life may be dealing you some exciting opportunities so be aware of what is going on around you. Be focused on your intentionality in order to transform your life, but not so focused that you miss the big opportunity staring you in the face.

Part C – Accountability and Advisors

One of the most successful techniques for implementing special projects or life change is to find a partner to hold you accountable for whatever you are doing. The benefit of an accountability partner is that he can keep you on track, give you encouragement, and help you resolve problems. Best of all, he can help you identify solutions.

Ten Rules For Accountability Relationships

1. The relationship should be open to all <u>related</u> questions. It is not necessarily open to every subject.
2. There are no secrets and no lying or cheating on answers. Total honesty is required. Answers should not understate or embellish.
3. Meet face-to-face at least once every month, weekly if possible.
4. Focus on fixing, not on blaming.
5. Set boundaries. Know what you want to achieve with the partner so draw lines or boundaries if they are needed.
6. Agree on the rules of confidentiality. In some cases it may be appropriate for the partners and the spouses to meet and agree up front on the rules of sharing conversations. This can also apply to other close members of the family.
7. The arrangement is not:

    *   sin management,
    *   a whipping post for mistakes,
    *   professional counseling,
    *   time for complaining and finger-pointing, or
    *   marriage counseling.

8. Talk and act in love. Gentleness is an important character trait for accountability partners.
9. Choose the accountability partner <u>carefully</u>. Consider gender, inter-personal skills, moral character, core values, intellectual ability, trustworthiness, age, interest in helping you, lack of personal agenda, and reputation.
10. Schedule a regular meeting, place, format, and agree on the rules.

Characteristics of an Accountability Arrangement

Choose <u>trusted</u> friends, not acquaintances for this important arrangement. Don't choose a "yes-man." You need someone who will tell you the truth in love. The arrangement could be one-way, with the partner asking questions and you answering. It could be a two-way arrangement where you ask each other questions. A two-way arrangement is more work and it may be more difficult to find a willing partner. We suggest a one-way arrangement unless the partner is doing something similar to what you are doing.

You can meet face-to-face or on your phone or computer . . . whatever works best. Face-to-face seems to work best for most people. The purpose is to help keep you on track but it can also help you make the right decisions. Be willing to ask for advice and counsel. There is usually an agreed-on list of questions that the partner will ask.

Advantages of an Accountability Arrangement

1. Meeting with someone else will prevent a feeling of isolation.

2. Talking often makes things clearer. When you ask questions or propose solutions out loud, clarification often occurs.

3. It's a safe place to discuss difficulties. Often others can see or detect what you cannot perceive.

4. It is protection for risk-takers. Sometimes you want to take risks that should be avoided.

5. It is a great weapon against apathy.

6. It encourages digging deeper into questions and issues that alone we would not face.

7. It keeps us actively engaged – knowing you will be talking to a partner about progress keeps you active.

8. It may help tear down walls that would otherwise remain without the help of a sounding board.

9. It helps draw a line in the sand if actions or thoughts get out of control, causing you to want to push the envelope.

What if it is not working?

Fix it, change it, or stop it.

What if I cannot find a good partner?

If you want help, consider our Coaching Assistance – see Chapter 15.

Chapter 13

Action Steps

"Action is a great restorer and builder of confidence.
Inaction is not only the result but the cause of fear.
Perhaps the action you take will be successful;
perhaps different action or adjustments will have to follow.
But any action is better than no action at all."
Norman Vincent Peale[63]

Introduction

Our overall goal is to live a better life. As we begin to identify specific action steps to achieve our Life Goals, it is worthwhile pausing to recognize the characteristics of _successful people_.

Here are nine characteristics that are common in successful people:

1. They focus their attitude and thoughts on success. They are positive and encouraging.

2. They look for solutions. They are not overly concerned about failures and missteps. They ignore insensitive disapproval.

3. They embrace change. They are not overwhelmed by it.

4. They think outside the box. They don't let the norms of life dictate decisions.

5. They are disciplined. They correct and regulate themselves.

6. They are intentional.

7. The exude confidence. They reject ignorance and fear.

8. They expect challenges and problems. They meet them head-on and conquer them.

9. They are industrious and keep their eyes on the goal.

> *"Everything you want is out there waiting for you to ask.*
> *Everything you want also wants you.*
> *But you have to take action to get it."*
> Jules Renard[64]

Actions, Strategies, and Plans

Keep the above characteristics in mind as you begin formulating actions steps you need to implement in order to accomplish your goals.

Your first decision is to consider how many of your Life Goals you are going to implement initially. Related to that question is, "Are you going to develop action steps for Goals you are not going to implement initially?" You could choose to develop actions steps for all your Life Goals and then only work on the top priority Goals. Thus, when you are ready to add new goals, the action steps will already be done.

There is no right or wrong decision here. Doing all the action steps now may be easier because it is all fresh in your mind. However, if you have a large number of Goals, you run the risk that your situation may change and the action steps are no longer applicable.

Chapter 12 – How To Do It

The previous chapter gives several important suggestions to help you implement change in your life. Before you proceed to develop your action steps, you should review Chapter 12 and list the suggestions you might consider using to accomplish your goals.

Look back and make note of the ideas you might want to implement. Space is provided here to briefly list eight ideas that you like:

1. _____

2. _____

3. _____

4. _____

5. _____

6. _____

7. _____

8. _____

As you progress through the process of developing action steps, remember these ideas and insert them where appropriate.

Space Provided

We have provided enough space for two Life Goals per planning category. If you have more goals or a long list of Action Steps, write those in the extra space provided, write them in a separate notebook, or enter them in your computer.

MY LIFE PLAN

PLANNING CATEGORY #1 – Life Principles and Attributes

Life Goal #1A:

_____

_____

Action Steps:

1A-a _____

1A-b _____

1A-c _____

1A-d _____

Life Goal #1B:

_____

_____

Action Steps:

1B-a _____

1B-b _____

1B-c _____

1B-d _____

MY LIFE PLAN

PLANNING CATEGORY #1 – Life Principles and Attributes

<u>Sample goals or action steps:</u>

<u>Honesty/Integrity:</u>
I will be honest, live with integrity, and live my life based on truth.
I will not compromise my integrity.
I will not steal anything from my employer, or anyone else.

<u>Other:</u>
I will diligently work at maintaining an outstanding reputation.
I will work at gaining the respect of others.
I will be authentic, genuine, and sincere.
I will seek knowledge, understanding, and wisdom.
I will choose my words carefully and always be in control of what I say and do.

+ _____ +

Space for additional notes, Life Goals, or Action Steps:

MY LIFE PLAN
PLANNING CATEGORY #2 – Habits

Life Goal #2A:

_____

_____

Action Steps:

2A-a _____

2A-b _____

2A-c _____

2A-d _____

Life Goal #2B:

_____

_____

Action Steps:

2B-a _____

2B-b _____

2B-c _____

2B-d _____

MY LIFE PLAN

PLANNING CATEGORY #2 – Habits

Sample goals or action steps:

Time Management:
I will better manage my time by:_____.

Rest/Relaxation:
I will spend more time relaxing by _____.
I will plan at least one family vacation each year

+ _____ +

Space for additional notes, Life Goals, or Action Steps:

MY LIFE PLAN
PLANNING CATEGORY #3 – Family and Relationships

Life Goal #3A:

_____

_____

Action Steps:

3A-a _____

3A-b _____

3A-c _____

3A-d _____

Life Goal #3B:

_____

_____

Action Steps:

3B-a _____

3B-b _____

3B-c _____

3B-d _____

MY LIFE PLAN
PLANNING CATEGORY #3 – Relationships

Sample goals or action steps:

Friends
I will choose my friends carefully.
I will be loyal to my friends, respecting and honoring their privacy and confidentiality.

Family & Marriage
I will include my family in all important life decisions.
I will have a "date night" each week with my spouse.
I will make every attempt to protect the dignity and quality of life of my parents as they age.

Sexual morality (fidelity/purity)
I will not cheat on my spouse.
I will save my virginity for my future husband/wife.

Teaching children:
I will establish and enforce reasonable rules for what our children watch and read, including TV, magazines, films, videos, computer, books, music, concerts, etc.
I will model appropriate behavior for my children.
I will be consistent in my discipline of my children.
I will teach my children that all actions have consequences.

+ _____ +

Space for additional notes, Life Goals, or Action Steps:

MY LIFE PLAN
PLANNING CATEGORY #4 – Work

Life Goal #4A:

_____

_____

Action Steps:

4A-a _____

4A-b _____

4A-c _____

4A-d _____

Life Goal #4B:

_____

_____

Action Steps:

4B-a _____

4B-b _____

4B-c _____

4B-d _____

MY LIFE PLAN
PLANNING CATEGORY #4 – Work

Sample goals or action steps:

Work ethic:
I will diligently do my job to the very best of my ability.
I will give a full day's work to my employer.
I will treat bosses/employees/co-workers with dignity and respect.
I will strive for excellence in my work.
I will not allow my work to define me.
I will not take a job that requires working on weekends/evenings/Sundays.
I will not regularly work more than 45 hours per week.

Type of work:
My work must be morally legitimate and useful to society.
I will not work for a business that makes (does) _____.

+ _____ +

Space for additional notes, Life Goals, or Action Steps:

MY LIFE PLAN
PLANNING CATEGORY #5 – Education

Life Goal #5A:

_____

_____

Action Steps:

5A-a _____

5A-b _____

5A-c _____

5A-d _____

Life Goal #5B:

_____

_____

Action Steps:

5B-a _____

5B-b _____

5B-c _____

5B-d _____

MY LIFE PLAN

PLANNING CATEGORY #5 – Education

Sample goals or action steps:

(Elementary, High School, College, Vocational, and Continuing Education)

I will complete my _____ education.
I will apply myself in order to have the grades I need to go to _____.
I will graduate in the top _____% of my class.
I will go to vocational school and learn to be a _____.
I will continue learning by attending _____.
I will read one new book each _____.
I will work an extra job in order to send my child to college.

+ _____ +

Space for additional notes, Life Goals, or Action Steps:

MY LIFE PLAN

PLANNING CATEGORY #6 – Community Service

Life Goal #6A:

_____

_____

Action Steps:

6A-a _____

6A-b _____

6A-c _____

6A-d _____

Life Goal #6B:

_____

_____

Action Steps:

6B-a _____

6B-b _____

6B-c _____

6B-d _____

MY LIFE PLAN
PLANNING CATEGORY #6 – Community Service

Sample goals or action steps:

I will volunteer my time at the local food bank.
I will volunteer my time at the local soup kitchen.
I will investigate local charities and volunteer my time and resources.
I will volunteer to pick up trash along a highway.
I will give _____% of my income each year to _____.
I will volunteer to read to the elderly.
I will volunteer to teach teenagers certain life skills.
I will rake the yard, mow grass, or perform repairs for my elderly neighbor.
I will teach adults new job skills.

+ _____ +

Space for additional notes, Life Goals, or Action Steps:

MY LIFE PLAN
PLANNING CATEGORY #7 – Money and Wealth

Life Goal #7A:

_____

_____

Action Steps:

7A-a _____

7A-b _____

7A-c _____

7A-d _____

Life Goal #7B:

_____

_____

Action Steps:

7B-a _____

7B-b _____

7B-c _____

7B-d _____

MY LIFE PLAN

PLANNING CATEGORY #7 – Money and Wealth

Sample goals or action steps:

Attitude/Lifestyle:
My lifestyle will be consistent with my level of income.
I will live within my means. I will not _____.
I will give a portion of my income to_____.
I will strive through good financial planning to legally minimize taxes.

Debt/ Credit/Lending:
I will strive to become and remain debt-free.
I will repay all debt on time and always pay off credit card balances on time.
I will limit credit card debt to _____.
I will not lend amounts that I cannot afford to lose.

Wealth Accumulation:
I will (will not) amass wealth for _____.
I will give away all excess wealth.
I will participate in my employer's 401k (savings) plan.

Inheritance:
I will limit, as appropriate, the absolute amount of wealth that I pass on to my children upon my death.

+ _____ +

Space for additional notes, Life Goals, or Action Steps:

MY LIFE PLAN
PLANNING CATEGORY #8 – Health

Life Goal #8A:

_____

_____

Action Steps:

8A-a _____

8A-b _____

8A-c _____

8A-d _____

Life Goal #8B:

_____

_____

Action Steps:

8B-a _____

8B-b _____

8B-c _____

8B-d _____

MY LIFE PLAN

PLANNING CATEGORY #8 – Health

Sample goals or action steps:

Lifestyle:
I will actively seek to maintain a healthy weight through proper diet and exercise.
I will not smoke or use recreational drugs.
I will not drink alcohol to excess.
I will get adequate sleep and rest.

Balance:
I am spending too much time_____; I will _____.
I am not giving enough time to_____; I will _____.

Attitude:
I will not worry, fret, or be anxious about _____.

Recreation/Enjoyment/Exercise/Sports:
I will begin _____.
I will stop_____.

\+ _____ +

Space for additional notes, Life Goals, or Action Steps:

MY LIFE PLAN

PLANNING CATEGORY #9 – Spiritual

Life Goal #9A:

_____

_____

Action Steps:

9A-a _____

9A-b _____

9A-c _____

9A-d _____

Life Goal #9B:

_____

_____

Action Steps:

9B-a _____

9B-b _____

9B-c _____

9B-d _____

MY LIFE PLAN

PLANNING CATEGORY #9 – Spiritual

Sample goals or action steps:

I will spend several hours each weekend seeking the truth about God.

I will spend 15 minutes per day in prayer.

I will intentionally learn about the tenets/doctrines of my faith.

+ _____ +

Space for additional notes, Life Goals, or Action Steps:

What Now?

Congratulations! You have basically completed drafting your Life Plan. Before you begin your Action Steps, there are four things you should know or remember:

1. Read the next chapter to gain an understanding of the importance of hope. Hope can set you free!

2. In Chapter 15 we outline the Life Coaching Services we provide. If you feel you need additional help in completing your plan or implementing your action plans we would be honored to help you. Jump ahead to the chapter after "Hope" for more details.

3. Remember to look at the subjects covered in the Appendices if you need further help in any of those subjects.

4. Lastly, note the other books and resources listed in "Next Steps" after the Appendices. Some of the Life Planning Series books may be directed at a particular subject that is important to you. These books will help you develop a plan to attack a particular issue, rather than the total Life Plan you have prepared in this book.

Our hope is that this book changes your life.

"Get action. Seize the moment.
Man was never intended to become an oyster."
Theodore Roosevelt[65]

Chapter 14

Hope and Encouragement

*What you place your hope in
will define the path for your life.*

General

In "*Animal Dreams*" Barbara Kingsolver writes, *"The very least you can do in your life is figure out what you hope for. And the most you can do is live inside that hope. Not admire it from a distance but live right in it, under its roof."*[66]

Hope is a very important component of our existence. You may not always be conscious of your hope, but it's what drives you forward; it is the inherent desire of your heart. It is often masked by other mental or emotional baggage, but it is there nevertheless.

Kingsolver's point is that we need to unmask that hope, embrace it, and intentionally bring it into our lives. We must not just think about it or admire it, but make it a part of our lives. Why? Because what we hope for will define the course of our lives. It defines what is ultimately important to us and it will shape our priorities.

What do you hope for?

MERRIAM-WEBSTER's definition of hope is to desire, with the expectation of obtaining the object of that desire. Genuine hope is not wishful thinking, but a firm assurance about things that are "unseen" and still in the future.

Hope looks ahead to a future expectation that is uplifting or optimistic. The opposite of hope is depression, sadness, or dejection. We can have different hopes for the many parts of our lives. Some are little hopes and others are large. Some may be huge. Lives can be built and lost on the nature of our hope.

What are your hopes? Take a few minutes before you proceed to think about and identify some of your hopes. What do you hope for? What hope sustains you? Are you conscious of your hopes? What hope would sustain you if you were living in dire circumstances? Jot some notes about your thoughts on "hope:"

_____

_____

_____

_____

_____

_____

_____

_____

_____

_____

_____

"Loyalty is what makes us trust.
Trust is what makes us stay.
Staying is what makes us love,
and love is what gives us hope."
Glenn van Dekken[67]

The Result of Hope

Many wise sayings about hope indicate that righteous people hope for joy or happiness but the destiny of wicked people is misery. What does it mean that the righteous hope for joy? Why joy? What is joy? Someone with joy has an inner peace, they are at rest, and they have a feeling of well-being. Typically joyful people are confident, assured, and have frequent feelings of happiness. If you asked them what or how they are feeling, they will often respond, "*Great!*"

Hope placed in evil and wickedness will not end well. Trouble is on the horizon, if it has not already arrived. Trouble, problems, and suffering are results of making bad choices, usually based on bad information, bad advice, or poor thinking.

Such trouble and suffering means loss, depression, mental anguish, lack of energy, and general despair. People often describe this feeling as "heartache." It can be said that this produces a broken spirit which can be debilitating because one feels lost, that no one cares, and life is not worthwhile. The <u>meaning</u> of life has been lost.

What meaning does life have for you?

> *"They say a person needs just three things*
> *to be truly happy in this world: someone to love,*
> *something to do, and something to hope for."*
> Tom Bodett[68]

Three Psychiatrists

In the period leading up to WW2 there were three Jewish psychiatrists: two learned masters in the field, and one young apprentice. The first master was a man named Sigmund Freud. He had spent years studying people, striving to understand what made people tick. He had reached the conclusion that the most basic drive in the human being was the drive for pleasure. He concluded that it is our need for pleasure that explains why we do what we do, how we live.

The second master was Alfred Adler. He too spent years studying human behavior. His studies led him to disagree with Sigmund Freud. Adler was convinced that the explanation for human behavior was power. All of us grow up feeling inferior and powerless. He concluded that life was a drive to gain control, to feel we are important.

The third man was a young up-and-coming psychiatrist by the name of Victor Frankl. He hoped to follow in the footsteps of his mentors. But before his career gained any momentum WW2 started. The Nazis invaded and life became dangerous for Jews. Freud and Adler were world renowned scholars and managed to escape before Hitler invaded. Frankl was not so lucky. He was arrested and thrown into a Nazi concentration camp for four long years.

After the war was over, Frankl was released from the concentration camp and resumed his career. As he reflected upon his time as a prisoner, he realized something quite strange: the people who survived were not always the ones you'd expect. Many who were physically strong wasted away and died. Others who were seemingly physically weak survived. Why? What was it that enabled them to hang on through a living hell?

Frankl reflected on the theories of his mentors. Freud's pleasure principle couldn't explain it. For desperate and terrible years the people in that camp knew only pain, suffering and degradation. Pleasure was not a word in their vocabulary. It wasn't pleasure that kept them going.

What then of Adler's theory about power being the basic human need? That didn't hold up well either. Frankl and his fellow Jews were completely powerless during their time in the concentration camps. Each day they stared down the barrels of loaded guns, were treated like animals, and suffered jackboots on their faces. They had no power and no prospect of power.

Victor Frankl came up with his own theory. The difference between those who survived and those who perished was *hope*. Those who survived never gave up their belief that their lives had meaning, that despite everything going on around them, this period would one day end and they would again live meaningful and purposeful lives.[69]

The one thing that gives life value, that gives us purpose, is that we live with a sense of hope and that our life has meaning. If there is no meaning in life, then why bother? Life reverts to chaos where there is no purpose and hope – no meaning. Do I exist to give myself pleasure and then disappear into the mist without meaning? Does that make any sense to you? There are people who believe that nonsense. I don't. I firmly believe that I exist because life does have meaning.

> *"Once you choose hope, anything's possible."*
> Christopher Reeve[70]

The Time is Now

Life goes by quickly. Elderly people looking back at their youth are particularly and poignantly aware of the passing years. The prime of life is fleeting. Thus it is wise not to put off until tomorrow what you can do today. The time is _now_. If you do it now you won't forget about it, and won't have to worry about getting it done before some deadline. You may even be able to enjoy the fruit of your labor.

This is good advice for everyone, but particularly important for those in the prime of life. We certainly have enough freedom in life to do most of the things we want and we should and can enjoy life. Although we are often told to follow our hearts, we also need to use wisdom in making good choices.

What is Your Hope?

List the most significant "hopes" in your life? Quiet your spirit and take time to really think about what you truly hope for. What are your life hopes? What are the deep desires of your heart?

_____

_____

_____

_____

_____

_____

_____

_____

_____

_____

_____

_____

Following are some possibilities:

1. that I am right with my God.
2. that I am a faithful and loving spouse or parent.
3. that I am a faithful and true leader in my family.
4. that I am a valued friend.
5. that my children and grandchildren have genuine joy in life.
6. that I use my skills, gifts, and resources wisely.
7. that I am honest and true, never misleading anyone.
8. that I serve my community well.
9. that my children will marry spouses who truly love them.
10. that I impact and improve someone's life.
11. that I have a life of good health.
12. that my family and extended family truly love one another.
13. that I will marry the love of my life.
14. that I will live to spoil my grandbabies.
15. that I will live to see my grandchildren marry.

Now go back to <u>your</u> list and identify the top five and prioritize them. How do your hopes fit with your Life Plan? Are they in harmony with your plans?

"Hope itself is like a star – not to be seen in the sunshine of prosperity, and only to be discovered in the night of adversity."

Charles H. Spurgeon[71]

Don't Hope in Wealth

If one or more of your hopes is in money or wealth, erase it, or cross it out. Destroy it! Hope placed in wealth fails. It is fleeting. It is fickle and it will not last. Hope in wealth comes from worldly values that disappear and can be lost forever at any time. The problem is we can tend to fall in love with money and the power it brings. Loving luxury, power, and wealth is at the root of much trouble.

The Source of Hope

Many proverbs and wise sayings identify the source of hope as "wisdom." Wisdom is permanent. It is extremely valuable because it can guide your decisions in life. Wisdom can give us a future so we have something to look forward to (to hope in). It will not fade away like a mist after a storm. It will not vanish in the face of trouble.

Wisdom will guide us in making right decisions.

Tips

ATTITUDES AND ACTIONS THAT ENCOURAGE HOPE:

- Be patient!
- Share your problems and difficulties with a trusted friend.
- Don't be constantly critical of life.
- Focus on what's important. Give little time to the little things.
- Understand that life has challenges. Everyone experiences tough times. You are not alone in that.
- Don't live in fear. Learn and grow from difficult times. Seek understanding from life situations.
- Be kind to yourself. Celebrate victories.
- Life is a journey, not a party.
- Be content with what you have.
- Be intentional: choose hope instead of fear.

TIPS FOR BEING HOPEFUL:

- Look on the bright side. Be an optimist, not a pessimist. Be positive and encourage others.
- Have an attitude of gratitude. Be a thankful person.
- See the humor in the human condition. Laugh at yourself. Don't take life too seriously.
- Listen to good music, read good books, watch good movies, and have good friends . . . (GIGO).
- Be healthy: take care of yourself physically (sleep, food, drink, and exercise).
- Avoid bad habits: alcohol, drugs, immorality, etc.
- Live and work in positive surroundings. Minimize exposure to negative influences.
- Have a life plan. Set goals. Know where you are going. Have a sense of purpose.
- Be organized. Have a to-do list and a schedule.

"Hope is medicine for a soul that's sick and tired."
Eric Swensson[72]

Chapter 15

Life Planning Coaching Assistance

NOTICE: Go to www.lifeplanningtools.com/coaching for complete details on the nature, cost, and availability of our Coaching Assistance.

At times we all need some help making a plan, getting motivated, or being held accountable. If you want that kind of assistance, please contact us. A general overview of our coaching assistance follows.

What We Will Do

We will provide help, guidance, and encouragement in:

1. Completing your Life Analysis.
2. Completing your Core Values, Priorities, and Commitments.
3. Completing your Personal Mission Statement.
4. Completing your Life Goals.
5. Completing your Action Steps.
6. Developing your entire Life Plan (beginning to end).
7. Implementing and monitoring your Life Plan.

What You Need to Do

Go to www.lifeplanningtools.com/coaching and complete the Application Form.

How Does It Work?

We will contact you to discuss our ability to assist you and give you any details you need in order to make a decision for our help. If you become a client, we will set up a schedule to talk with you by phone or online.

How Long Does It Last?

As long as you desire. You may terminate our help at any time. See the website for details.

What Will It Cost?

Go to www.lifeplanningtools.com/coaching for details, or scan the QR code below.

Appendix A: Christian Perspective

"If you love me, obey my commandments. And I will ask the Father, and he will give you another Advocate, who will never leave you. He is the Holy Spirit, who leads into all truth. The world cannot receive him, because it isn't looking for him and doesn't recognize him. But you know him, because he lives with you now and later will be in you."
(John 14:15-17 NLT)

Introduction

This Appendix is written for the Christian believer relative to developing this Life Plan. It will also provide the non-Christian insight about the Christian faith. If you are curious about Christian faith principles and how a Christian might approach this planning process, please read through this Appendix.

Our purpose is to give the Christian guidance in using this Planning Handbook because the Handbook is written from a secular perspective. In other words, the Life Plan does not assume a religious position.

It does, however, include a "Spiritual" category in developing your Life Goals in Chapter 8.9. If you are a Christian, you may have reached that section in the planning process and are wondering what you should do. We will provide you further guidance in the following pages.

Our plan is to go through each of the major subjects of core values, priorities, commitments, goals, and your personal mission statement and provide you with tips and advice as to what to consider as you prepare and finalize these areas of your Life Plan.

Personal Mission Statement

If you are a Christian you should begin with your Personal Mission Statement, because it will impact all the other subjects. This is especially true of your Core Values, which in this Handbook occur before the Mission Statement. If you are a committed Christian or even a casual believer, you should prepare your preliminary mission statement first.

The mission statement of Christians <u>may</u> have a strong religious perspective. As a Christian your mission statement would not necessarily be focused on your faith, but if it is, you might have a mission statement like one of the following:

> 1. To have a vibrant, personal, growing relationship with God through Jesus and the Holy Spirit by optimizing the use of my God-given talents, resources, and spiritual gifts to help others grow in their faith.

> 2. To cooperate with Christ in conforming me to His likeness, using all my resources to serve Him, my family, and others through my work and service to my church

> 3. To obey God's commission to make and teach disciples.

> 4. To be an example of Christ through my work and perseverance, exhibiting a Christ-like attitude to all my fellow workers and business associates.

> 5. To be a student of the Bible, reading, studying, and teaching, in order to teach and communicate the Word of God to others.

Alternatively, it might be a very simple statement like: *To make Jesus Christ the central reality of my life.*

The important point is that a Christian-focused mission statement will have *great impact* on your Core Values, Priorities, and Commitments. As a Christian you probably want your mission (life purpose) to rightly impact your values, priorities, and commitments in order that you are accomplishing the objectives God has planned for your life.

If you are a casual believer, this may sound like it is way beyond your comfort zone or just not where you are at this time in your life. That's fine. You should determine if you want any faith perspective in your personal mission statement and then take any faith issues or questions to Chapter 8.9 where you can address any Spiritual Goals.

Alternatively you might consider some combination of a faith and worldly purpose.

Core Values

If you are a Christian, you might want to include one or two core values related to your faith. Remember, core values are the standards by which you live. They reflect what you believe in. What Christian values or standards will you absolutely not compromise or violate? These are your core values.

Core values are important because they will guide you in many important decisions and help you choose your direction. Possible Christian subjects that you might consider for core values are:

- Believing in the power of prayer.
- Believing in the truth of the Bible.
- Relying on the power of the Holy Spirit to live the Christian life.
- Knowing your hope is in Christ alone.
- Understanding you are a sinner saved by grace.
- Knowing you are being conformed to the likeliness of Christ.
- Believing Jesus is the Lord of your life.
- Believing Jesus has paid your sin debt.

Priorities

Given your Christian-related Mission Statement and Core Values, what priorities relative to your Christian faith do you have or should you have? The answer will obviously be totally dependent on your personal circumstances and where you are in your Christian life.

You might consider the following and determine if they are priorities or goals in your life:

1. **Intentional Obedience**: I will intentionally commit my life to be obedient to God's Word.

2. **Intimate Worship**: I will earnestly seek to worship in spirit and truth; I will celebrate the majesty of God's Name!

3. **Spiritual Growth**: I will zealously meditate on and study the Word of God.

4. **Fervent Prayer**: I will diligently pray for personal transformation, for the church, for the hurting, and for the lost.

5. **Humble Service**: I will humbly serve God by actively serving people in true loving kindness. I will faithfully use my gifts, talents, and skills in ministry, serving God and His church.

6. **Thankful Giving**: I will tithe to my local church and share with those in need.

7. **Intentional Faith-based Conversations:** I will actively pursue conversations about God's truth with others.

8. **Committed Relationships**: I will encourage and be accountable to other Christ-followers.

9. **Faithful Attendance**: I will faithfully and regularly attend my local church. I will be an active participant, offering my gifts and skills in His service.

10. **Divine Power**: I will passionately seek His presence and power in my life in order to accomplish all of the above.

You can use the above listing for either priorities or goals. Simply rewrite them to fit your needs. You might begin by identifying the top three subjects above and then determine if any of them warrant being a Life Priority in your current circumstances.

Commitments

Remember, your Life Commitments are those commitments that must be made in order to achieve your Personal Mission and Life Priorities. In many cases the difference between a goal and a commitment might be rather small. What Christian commitments must you make in order to accomplish your desired legacy, dreams, Core Values, Life Priorities, and ultimately your Life Mission?

First, revisit your priorities above and determine if any of these subjects should be one of your Life Priorities. The sentences following the subject are written in the form of a commitment statement and might be used with personal modification.

Then review your Mission Statement and Core Values to determine if there are other obvious commitments you should include in order to accomplish your Life Mission.

Life Goals

Based on everything you did above, your Christian Life Goals should be obvious to you. Integrate the information above into the process in Chapter 8.9 and develop your final Life Goals in the Spiritual Category of your Life Plan.

Conclusion/Summary

We hope that you are comfortable with what you developed above. If you have been struggling with your faith, you may have questions that are beyond the scope of this book.

The Christian faith is relatively simple and easy to understand. It is you and I who create the difficulties, often because we do not have a clear understanding of the basic tenets of the faith. It may have never been clearly explained to you or you may have been too busy to hear and understand the gospel message.

The basic principles of the Christian faith are quite simple:

1. Man is inherently sinful. Our sin (rebellion against God) has separated us from God. Thus, we cannot have a personal relationship with Him.

> *For ever since the world was created, people have seen the earth and sky. Through everything God made, they can clearly see his invisible qualities—his eternal power and divine nature. So they have no excuse for not knowing God. Yes, they knew God, but they wouldn't worship him as God or even give him thanks. And they began to think up foolish ideas of what God was like. As a result, their minds became dark and confused. Claiming to be wise, they instead became utter fools. 23 And instead of worshiping the glorious, ever-living God, they worshiped idols made to look like mere people and birds and animals and reptiles. (Ro 1:20-23 NLT)*

2. We are incapable of fixing our sin problem. No one is righteous and no one can be declared righteous because of his good deeds or works. We cannot earn our way back into the good graces of a holy God.

> *For no one can ever be made right with God by doing what the law commands. The law simply shows us how sinful we are. (Ro 3:20 NLT)*

3. Therefore, God Himself made a way to reconcile us to Himself by sending His Son Jesus to pay the debt for our sin through the shedding of His blood (death).

> *We are made right with God by placing our faith in Jesus Christ. And this is true for everyone who believes, no matter who we are. For everyone has sinned; we all fall short of God's glorious standard. Yet God, with undeserved*

kindness, declares that we are righteous. He did this through Christ Jesus when he freed us from the penalty for our sins. (Ro 3:22-24 NLT)

But God showed his great love for us by sending Christ to die for us while we were still sinners. (Ro 5:8 NLT)

For the wages of sin is death, but the free gift of God is eternal life through Christ Jesus our Lord. (Ro 6:23 NLT)

4. Jesus is our way back into the grace of God, and He is the only way.

> *Jesus told him, "I am the way, the truth, and the life. No one can come to the Father except through me."* (John 14:6 NLT)

5. It is by the <u>grace</u> of God that we are saved. We cannot earn it. It is a gift from God

> *God saved you by his grace when you believed. And you can't take credit for this; it is a gift from God. Salvation is not a reward for the good things we have done, so none of us can boast about it.* (Eph 2:8-9 NLT)

6. But we must believe and receive the gift.

> But to all who believed him and accepted him, he gave the right to become children of God. (John 1:12 NLT)

7. What is required on our part? We must believe in our <u>heart</u>, and confess our sin.

> If you confess with your mouth that Jesus is Lord and believe in your heart that God raised him from the dead, you will be saved. For it is by believing in your heart that you are made right with God, and it is by confessing with your mouth that you are saved. (Ro 10:9-10 NLT)

8. We must turn to God.

> Look! I stand at the door and knock. If you hear my voice and open the door, I will come in, and we will share a meal together as friends. (Rev 3:20 NLT)

9. We receive Christ by faith. We intentionally make that choice. Our decision is made based on God's promises, our trust in His Word, and not on feelings and emotions.

> Those who accept my commandments and obey them are the ones who love me. And because they love me, my Father will love them. And I will love them and reveal myself to each of them. (John 14:21 NLT)

10. You are a child of God.

> But to all who believed him and accepted him, he gave the right to become children of God. (John 1:12 NLT)

As we said, this is a pretty simple concept. That is why children can be saved when they are old enough to understand, believe, and receive His grace. The more amazing part of this is what happens to the true believer (those who believe in their heart). The following is a description of the Christian believer.

> I am part of the family of God.
> I am a child of the King.
> I am a son of the Most High.
> I am a brother to the Savior.
> I am a sheep in the flock of the Great Shepherd.
> I am a joint-heir with Christ to the Kingdom of God.
> I am a priest in the priesthood of Christ, who is the High Priest.
> I am a member of the Body of Christ.
> I am a new creation of the Creator.
> I am a bride of the Bridegroom.
> I am a servant of the Master.
> I am clay in the hands of the Potter.
> I am redeemed by the Lamb.
> I am a part of His house in which He is the Cornerstone.
> I am a branch of the Vine.
> I am reconciled to the Healer.
> I am a saint of the Holy One.
> I am a disciple of the Teacher.
> I am a child of the King.
> I am a son of the Most High.
> I am a brother to the Savior.
> I am a joint-heir with Christ to all the promises of God.

because

> I am redeemed by the Lamb and
> I am part of the family of God.

FEAR

Michelle Berkey-Hill is an artist and writer. You can see her work at: www.graceandthegravelroad.com. In 2019, she participated in a ten-day mission trip to Guatemala, where she used her art to encourage young children in a very poor area of the country. Upon her return, she sent out a news update.

The subject of her message was "fear," and her words immediately hit home as I was thinking about the challenge of being intentional. She was right on target for those struggling with the fear of being intentional.

HER ORIGINAL MESSAGE:

> *I'm dealing with a constant barrage of small fears this week. We leave for a missions trip on Friday. When this is published, we'll be in the midst of team training and prep in Guatemala (God willing). The week before leaving on a trip like this is grueling. I'm wavering between the "what the heck I was thinking" and the "I'll never be ready" phases of preparing for the trip!*

> *We've had a full week even if we weren't planning to leave. Landscape blocks were delivered. Because they'll kill the lawn if we let them sit there for a few weeks, we found ourselves testing sprinkler locations and building a retaining wall at 10:30 pm. Today, plants that go inside that wall arrive. When I ordered them, I thought they'd arrive a week ago. They're bare root plants. They won't survive two weeks unless I put them in some dirt somewhere. My boyfriend, Tim, is coming on the trip as well, but he's spending today traveling to and from a funeral instead of packing and prepping as we expected.*

> *The reality is that it'll all get done. I might not get as much sleep as I'd prefer, but what really has to get done will get done. In the midst of the crazy preparations, packing, building retaining walls, and testing my workshop lessons, these are the thoughts which have battered my mind this week:*

> *What was I thinking? I must have been crazy.*
> *I don't have anything valuable to offer.*

How can one who struggles to call herself an artist, teach art?
I've never taught art before. I can't do this.
This is totally unfamiliar, how am I going to deal with this?
I don't know what I'm doing.
This will never work.
I'm too old. I don't know enough.
I'm not physically up to it (I have a back and a shoulder injury).
I have no idea if the kids will be able to do this project.
This was a big mistake.

There's a big difference between the theoretical and the actual. The idea of a missions trip is amazing. Thinking about the thing God's told you to do is wonderful. Actually doing it is a whole different thing. It's harder, messier, and less certain. But, he doesn't ask you to think about the thing he wants you to do, he asks you to do it. And he doesn't ask you to do it alone.

The root of all my objections above is fear.

The answer to that fear is, "But, God." But God can. God will.

God has all of it covered, no matter what it looks like. I know that and this week I'm having to choose to walk in that knowledge every single moment.

I can't, but God can. This is a real thing, not a pretty sentiment to print on a coffee mug and entertain yourself with. This is an in-the-trenches "use it" kind of phrase. How do you need to practice "But, God" this coming week?

[Written June 16, 2019 by Michelle Berkey-Hill for *Soul Shaper*]

TWO WEEKS LATER:

"Two weeks ago, I wrote you a note about fear. Fear was creeping around the edges of my heart and slithering in every crack they could find because I was about to embark on something new. Something different. Something out of my comfort zone. I was about to leave on a mission trip to a place I'd

never been, where I didn't speak the language, and I was going to serve in a capacity I've never served. I love to travel, I was excited about this trip, and I knew intellectually that it would all work out. But, that didn't stop fear from trying to derail me. My answer to all those fears was, "But, God."

I can't, but God can.

I don't know how this will all work out, but God does.

I have no control over how well this unfolds, but God does.

And I can rest in that, because God is bigger than all that I venture into.

> "Little children, you are from God and have overcome them, for He who is in you is greater than he who is in the world." (1 John 4:4)

Faith dispels fear. There is something else that dispels fear as well. Action.

Usually, I prepare these emails in advance, but today, I'm writing this to you on this beautiful Sunday morning from a hotel room safely back in the US after an unforgettable two weeks. I'm thinking back over the events since I wrote that email about fear and I'm realizing that once the alarm rang at 4 am on the morning we left for the airport, the fears dissipated. There was no time for them. Action took all of my attention.

Movement in the direction of your goal quiets the fears that come before you start. Not that the trip was all rainbows and butterflies, it wasn't. But, those fears that come before you begin a new thing, the "I can't", the "what if it doesn't work" and the "this is the dumbest thing I've ever done" are all silenced by the doing.

So, if there's something you're about to begin. If there's a new thing on your horizon. If God's asking you to do something. And you're feeling the fear. Know that there are two tools you can use *to combat those fears. Faith and action. And once you get past the starting gate, Fear has failed and you will be on your way.*

You see, there will always be fear before adventure. Fear before success. Fear before a journey. Fear wants to keep you in a small little comfortable tightly controlled container. But a full life with all its beauty and adventure is outside of that container. Sure, there may be bruises and setbacks along the way. But, as I looked into the unwavering gaze of a Mayan boy and told him how much God loves him and that he is an amazing work of art, all the bruises and setbacks are forgotten and there is only God's love for people that matters.

What one small thing can you do this week to step toward the thing that you're afraid of?

I cannot think of any better advice or encouragement. Maybe you can't do it, but God can. He may have even provided you some friends that will help and support you. If not, then He alone is enough.

If you want to be all you can be, now is the time!

INSTRUCTION TO CHRISTIANS:

We recommend that you read and do Chapter 5 before doing Chapter 4.

Appendix B – How to Prioritize

Identify what is important to you and do it first.

GENERAL

What are your objectives? Ask yourself:

1. What's most important, considering my responsibilities and goals?

2. How can I make the most significant contribution?

You will need to be relentless in sticking to your priorities. Like your life and career, your priorities will change and evolve over time. Setting priorities takes some time but it will pay off in productivity.

The key is working on things that really make a difference. Does this make a difference for my family? Does this make friends or co-workers happy? Does this impact my life in any positive way? What difference am I making and at the end of the day can I feel good about the result?

General questions to think about and guide the process:

- What needs to be done _now_?
- What is most important among a number of possibilities?
- What happens if it doesn't get done?
- When do I need to begin in order to finish on time?
- What materials, resources and skills do I need to accomplish the objective?

It is imperative that you track your progress. What is the current status of your plans or projects? What is getting done? How much have you completed? What is not getting done? Why? Does something need to change in order to make progress? What priorities need to be changed?

The Process

1. MAKE A LIST

Write a list of all your tasks. Identify the due dates for the tasks, if applicable. It is important to maintain an up-to-date list and also wise to keep an electronic back-up of the master list. Your master to-do list serves as a running log of what you want to accomplish over time. Because your master list can change, it may be convenient to manage and update it in a digital format.

2. ASSIGN STATUS

Categorize your tasks into:

Do Now: Very important. I need to work on this now.
Prioritize: These tasks need to be prioritized.
Delete: These should be removed from my list.

3. TIME FRAME

Assign an appropriate timeframe. For example, this task needs to be accomplished:
       a. today.
       b. this week.
       c. this month.
       d. this quarter.
Identify the date you want to begin.

4. EFFORT

Assign each task an estimated effort. How many hours, days, or weeks will be required to complete the task? Be realistic about how much work you can actually do. Tasks often take longer than expected. Interruptions come up. Days get filled with distractions.

5. URGENCY/IMPORTANCE/PRIORITY

Identify "urgent" versus "important." Ignore anything else unless your list is <u>very</u> short. Here are three approaches. Choose one.

a. Scale Method: On a scale of 1 to 10 assess value or importance.

b. The Eisenhower Matrix Method:

Urgent and Important:	Do these tasks as soon as possible.
Not urgent, but important:	Decide when you'll do these.
Urgent, but not important:	Delegate these tasks to someone else.
Not urgent nor important:	Drop these from your schedule as soon as possible.

c. The Pareto Principle (80/20 rule)
    20% of your efforts tend to produce 80% of your results.
    Where will you get the biggest bang for your buck?
    Work on the 20% portion first.

d. Other Simple Strategies
    Do the most important task first.
    Do the most impactful task first.
    Complete one major important task at a time.
    Find the key PARETO tasks.
    Do a simple high/medium/low assignment.

6. FLEXIBILITY

Be flexible. Situations and circumstances can change very quickly. Reevaluate your priority list frequently. If priorities change stop, reassess, and move on to the next priority.

7. TIME TO STOP

Know when to stop working on a goal or action step. Make sure that what you are doing warrants your time. Stop what you are doing, fix what is wrong if necessary, and move on.

8. DANGERS

    a. Perfection: You seek perfection. Know when you are done.

    b. Procrastination: You can't seem to get started.

    c. Inflexible: You don't recognize that you should change what you are doing.

Tips For Being More Effective

- Bundle similar tasks together.
- Start a task and work on it until it is done.
- Allocate time to do work on your priority list and calendar.
- Work on one thing at a time.
- Don't put action steps off until the last minute.
- Take breaks to refresh your heart and mind.
- Follow up with people who are helping you.
- Anticipate changes, challenges, problems, delays, etc.

Appendix C - Scheduling

Your time is precious.

Whether you are a stay-at-home mom or the CEO of a large corporation you need a calendar. You must schedule your meetings, appointments, dates, phone calls, projects, etc.

We put this short subject in an Appendix of its own because it is vital to your success. It doesn't make any real difference what process or techniques you use. You can write it on your bathroom mirror if that works for you. But you must make a habit of entering your schedule on your calendar.

If you are over age 16 you have a schedule that you must keep. Many college freshmen learn this the hard way when they show up on campus. The professors assume they can follow simple directions and record in some organized manner what and when assignments are due.

In every walk of life some portion of your success will depend on how well you keep track of your schedule. If you don't show up or if you are always late, you won't hold down a job very long. If you are trying to live a better life, you need a planner, calendar, or schedule to alert you to where you are supposed to be and what you are supposed to be doing.

Time may be your most valuable asset. Treat it that way! If you want to accomplish anything significant, you must have a scheduling system that is your friend. You should not only schedule your tasks but also your times of relaxation. Put on your calendar all the pertinent information necessary to accomplish your Life Plan Action Steps.

That's it. Get a calendar and use it.

Appendix D – Decision-Making

**"Unintended consequences rush us recklessly through life,
allowing no time for perspective."**
Unknown[73]

Making Choices

People who work at staying on their path with their eyes fixed on the goal are less likely to make wrong or poor decisions. Why? They have an advantage because they are actively thinking about choices and are aware of the consequences of those choices.

There are many major decisions in life: (a) choosing friends, (b) choosing schools and colleges, (c) choosing a spouse, (d) choosing a career or accepting a job; (e) buying a house, (f) investing in a business, etc. In addition, we make many other simple choices daily, like when to get up, what to wear, whether to exercise, or what to eat.

*"The most difficult thing is the decision to act,
the rest is merely tenacity. The fears are paper tigers.
You can do anything you decide to do.
You can act to change and control your life;
and the procedure, the process is its own reward."*
Amelia Earhart[74]

People make decisions in a number of different ways. Some people tend to rely on instinct or intuition. They just "feel" what the right thing is to do. Others gather data and information, filling notebooks with everything they can think of that would help determine the right decision. Some make a check list of every question and answer before they decide. Others use the trusted "pros and cons" approach.

We tend to favor an analytical approach to making important decisions. This requires looking at a number of different factors before making a decision. Some of these factors will not apply to every question or to your particular situation. Just ignore those; they may be useful later.

METHOD: Short and Sweet

Some of you will want to make this process short and sweet. If you are one of those people, the following eight questions may be adequate for you to make a good decision.

1. Do I want to do it or not do it?
2. Would it violate a worldly law or a precept of God?
3. Does it violate my integrity in any way (or my core values)?
4. Would it damage my reputation, if known?
5. Would it impact others or be hurtful to anyone in any way?
6. If I can answer all the above "no," then what are the pros and cons?
7. What will I gain and what do I risk?
8. After weighing the pros and cons and understanding the risk/reward, ask, "What is the best alternative?"

TEN STEPS TO GOOD DECISIONS

1. DEFINE IT: Obtain _all_ the necessary information and state the question or problem in a simple, understandable, clear sentence or two.

2. LEGAL or ETHICAL: Does this decision involve any (a) legal issues, (b) ethical standards, (c) moral boundaries, or (d) company rules and policies? Clarify in detail.

3. CONSEQUENCES: What are the potential consequences? Can I live with them? Who and what will be affected, influenced, or impacted?

4. RISKS and REWARDS: What are the potential risks and rewards? What can I gain or lose? Are the risks reasonable?

5. EXPERTISE: Do I have the skill and wisdom to make this decision?

6. ADVISORS: Seek out advisors to provide helpful and honest advice.

7. PERSONAL CONSIDERATIONS: Does this fit my spiritual standards? Is it consistent with my core values and life goals? Do I have a passion or vision for this issue or project? Are my motives right? Am I being influenced by feelings, emotions, fears, or insecurities?

8. ALTERNATIVE SOLUTIONS: Take time to fully analyze the information in order to make a fully informed decision based on analyzing several viable alternatives.

9. DECIDE: Verify the facts, think about and study the solution, and make the decision.

10. AFTERWARD: Your work is just beginning! Now that the decision is made, monitor the situation closely so that the intended result occurs. Take corrective action as needed.

You can obtain a FREE expanded version of this Appendix!
It's 20+ pages and will provide a detailed outline of
how to make wise decisions.

Go to www.lifeplanningtools.link/howtodecide
for your free PDF copy, or scan the QR code below.

Get a Kindle ebook version for $0.99 at:

https://www.amazon.com/dp/B09SYGWRVL/

NEXT STEPS

LIFE PLANNING SERIES

Should you read any books in this series? That depends on your interest and objectives. If you want to gain specific knowledge about a particular subject, then the answer is "yes." If you want to improve your life and concentrate on a particular area, again the answer is "yes."

We have listed the books and the planned topics again. Please note that this list will not be final or up-to-date until the last book in the Series is published.

RECOMMENDATION: We strongly recommend that if you acquire any of the books you obtain _Choose Integrity_. This is the foundational book in the series. We also believe the books covering the other Primary Life Principles would be particularly useful: Friends, Speech, Diligence, and Money.

The initial plan is to publish books on the following topics:

Subjects		Life Principle
Personal Character:		
Integrity*	honesty, truth, compromise/standing firm, justice, fairness	Be honest, live with integrity, and base Life on truth.
Reputation	respect, responsibility, sincerity	Earn the respect of others.
Leadership	power, decisiveness, courage, influence, loyalty	Lead well and be a loyal follower.
Identity/Self-Image	humor, being genuine, authenticity, confidence	Be confident in who you are.
Wisdom	discernment, correction, folly, foolishness	Seek knowledge, understanding, and wisdom.
Personal Relationships:		
Friends*	Friends, associates, acquaintances	Choose your friends wisely.
Family	Honor, parenting, discipline	Honor your family.
Love	Love is . . .	Love one another.

Compassion	humility, mercy, goodness, kindness	Treat others as you would want to be treated.
Forgiveness	reject grudges and revenge	Forgive others; do not hold grudges or take revenge.

Self-Control:

Speech*		Guard your speech.
Anger	self-control, self-discipline, patience	Always be under control.
Addiction	moderation, life balance	Live a life of balance and moderation, not excess.
Immorality	temptation	Set high moral standards.

Work Ethic:

Diligence*	apathy, laziness, perseverance, resilience, energy	Be diligent and a hard worker.
Trustworthiness	dependability, reliability, responsibility	Be trustworthy, dependable, and reliable.
Skills	curiosity, knowledge, education, abilities	Seek excellence; strive to do everything well.

Wealth:

Money*	wealth, poverty	Make sound financial choices.
Gratitude	generosity, thankfulness, gratefulness	Be thankful, grateful, and generous.
*The first subject listed under each of the categories above make up the Primary Life Principles.		

After the initial launch the books will be published in 4 to 8 week intervals.

SUPPLEMENTAL BOOKS

(Available after the Life Planning Series is published)

> ***Daily Encouragement*** (250 short reviews on topics from the Life Planning Series)

> ***Table Talk*** (Questions and answers for dinner table discussion)

CHRISTIAN WISDOM SERIES

> Because the Christian perspective on many of these subjects is unique, we have planned a Christian Wisdom Series that will examine the Christian view on most of the subjects in the Life Planning Series. This series is planned for release after the Life Planning Series is published.

COACHING ASSISTANCE

See Chapter 15 for an outline of our assistance or scan QR to go to details on our website.

Life Planning Series

The Primary Life Principles

You Can Change Your Life!

CHOOSE INTEGRITY	**Life Principle:** Be honest, live with integrity, and base your life on truth.
CHOOSE FRIENDS WISELY	**Life Principle:** Choose your friends wisely.
CHOOSE THE RIGHT WORDS	**Life Principle:** Guard your speech.
CHOOSE GOOD WORK HABITS	**Life Principle:** Be diligent and a hard worker.
CHOOSE FINANCIAL RESPONSIBILITY	**Life Principle:** Make sound financial choices.
SCAN ME	**Scan the Q/R code to the left with your phone to check on availability of all books in the Life Planning Series. These five will be published in 2022.**

Free PDF

Wise Decision-Making

[Get the ebook version for 99 cents]

We want to give you a <u>free</u> copy of:

Wise Decision-Making: You can make good choices.

This book will help you make good decisions in your life, career, family . . .

Free PDF:
www.lifeplanningtools.link/howtodecide

eBook for 99 cents:
https://www.amazon.com/dp/B09SYGWRVL/

Ebook

Free PDF

Acknowledgments

My wife has patiently persevered while I indulged my interest in this subject. Thank you for your patience.

Our older daughter has been an invaluable resource. She has also graciously produced our website at www.lifeplanningtools.com

Our middle daughter designed all the covers for this series. We are very grateful for her help, talent and creativity.

Notes

QUOTES

ACCURACY: We have used a number of quotes throughout this book that came from our files, notes, books, public articles, the Internet, etc. We have made no attempt to verify that these quotes were actually written or spoken by the person they are attributed to. Regardless of the source of these quotes, the wisdom of the underlying message is relative to the content in this book and worth noting, even if the source reference is erroneous.

SOURCE: Unless otherwise specifically noted below the quotes used herein can be sourced from a number of different websites on the Internet that provide lists of quotes by subject or author. The same or similar quotes will appear on multiple sites. Therefore, rather than assign individual quote sources, we are providing a list of sites where we might have found the quotes that were used in this book:

--azquotes.com
--brainyquote.com
--codeofliving.com
--everydaypower.com
--goodhousekeeping.com
--goodreads.com/quotes
--graciousquotes.com
--inc.com
--keepinspiring.me
--notable-quotes.com
--parade.com
--plantetofsuccess.com
--quotemaster.org
--quotir.com
--success.com
--thoughtco.com
--thoughtcatalog.com
--wisdomquotes.com
--wisesayings.com
--wow4u.com

1 Nelson Mandela, see QUOTES above.
2 Archibald Marwizi, see QUOTES above.
3 Abraham Lincoln, see QUOTES above.
4 Albert Einstein, see QUOTES above.
5 Patrick Ness, see QUOTES above.
6 Thomas Edison, see QUOTES above.
7 Paul Coelho, see QUOTES above.
8 Jim Rohn, see QUOTES above.
9 Josh McDowell, *Evidence That Demands A Verdict*, Thomas Nelson
   publisher, ISBN: 9781401676704.
10 Latin American saying, see QUOTES above.
11 Aesop, see QUOTES above.

12 SermonCentral.com; contributed by Perry Greene

13 Buddha, see QUOTES above.

14 Honoré de Balzac, see QUOTES above.

14.5 A large number of Internet sites. Search for "Jonathan Edwards," "Max Jukes," or "A. E. Winship."

15 Lysa Terkeurst, *The Best Yes,* Thomas Nelson Publisher, ISBN: 978-1-4002-02585-1

16 Cicero, see QUOTES above.

17 Unknown, see QUOTES above.

18 Don Shula, see QUOTES above.

19 Unknown, see QUOTES above.

20 Stephen Covey, see QUOTES above.

21 Archibald Marwizi, see QUOTES above.

22 Kenneth Blanchard, see QUOTES above.

23 Ronald Reagan, see QUOTES above.

24 Brian Tracy, see QUOTES above.

25 Les Brown, see QUOTES above.

26 Lou Holtz, see QUOTES above.

27 George Bernard Shaw, see QUOTES above.

28 Martin Luther King Jr., see QUOTES above.

29 Norman Vincent Peale, see QUOTES above.

30 George Bernard Shaw, see QUOTES above.

31 John C. Maxwell, see QUOTES above.

32 Tonny Rutakirwa, see QUOTES above.

33 Dale Carnegie, see QUOTES above.

34 Bible, Book of Ecclesiastes 3:12-13.

35 Vince Lombardi, see QUOTES *above.*

36 Vince Lombardi, see QUOTES above.

36.5 Henry Ford, see QUOTES above.

37 Albert Schweitzer, see QUOTES above.

38 George Bernard Shaw, *The Meaning of Life in 15 Wise Quotes,* by SUCCESS Staff, Oct 12, 2017.

39 Unknown, see QUOTES above.

40 Edmund Burke, see QUOTES above.

41 Richard M. DeVos, see QUOTES above.

42 Will Rogers, see QUOTES above.

43 Tammy Taylor, see QUOTES above.

44 Thomas Jefferson, see QUOTES above.

45 Paulo Coelho, see QUOTES above.

46 Mahatma Gandhi, see QUOTES above.

47 Oscar Wilde, see QUOTES above.

48 Maya Angelou, see QUOTES above.

49 Dalai Lama, see QUOTES above.

50 Ralph Waldo Emerson, see QUOTES above.

51 Lao Tzu, see QUOTES above.

52 Mary Engelbreit, see QUOTES above.

53 Josh Billings, see QUOTES above.

54 Thomas Jefferson, see QUOTES above.

55 Maxime Lagacé, see QUOTES above.

56 Carrie Green, see QUOTES above.

57 Bible: Book of 1 Kings 3:9

58 Joel Annesley, see QUOTES above.

59 Thomas A. Edison, see QUOTES above.

60 Billy Graham, see QUOTES above.

61 George Bernard Shaw, see QUOTES above.

62 Vince Lombardi, see QUOTES above.

63 Norman Vincent Peale, see QUOTES above.

64 Jules Renard, see QUOTES above.

65 Theodore Roosevelt, see QUOTES above.

66 Barbara Kingsolver. *Animal Dreams*, Harper Perennial; Reissue edition (2013), ISBN-13: 978-0062278500.

67 Glenn van Dekken, see QUOTES above.

68 Tom Bodett, see QUOTES above.

69 Victor Frankl, Based on a talk given by Australian speaker Michael Frost.

70 Christopher Reeve, see QUOTES above.

71 Charles H. Spurgeon, see QUOTES above.

72 Eric Swensson, see QUOTES above.

73 Unknown, see QUOTES above.

74 Amelia Earhart, see QUOTES above.

Bible Translation Used

Scriptures marked NLT are taken from the HOLY BIBLE, NEW LIVING TRANSLATION (NLT): Scriptures taken from the HOLY BIBLE, NEW LIVING TRANSLATION, Copyright© 1996, 2004, 2007 by Tyndale House Foundation. Used by permission of Tyndale House Publishers, Inc., Carol Stream, Illinois 60188. All rights reserved. Used by permission.

About the Author

The author graduated from the Business School at Indiana University and obtained a master's degree at Georgia State University in Atlanta. His first career was as a senior executive with a top insurance and financial institution, where he spent a number of years directing strategic planning for one of their major divisions.

In the 1990s he founded an online Internet business which he sold in 2010. He began to write and publish books and materials that led to an interest in personal life planning. This resulted in combining the wisdom of wise sayings and proverbs with life planning and the result is the Life Planning Series and the Life Planning Handbook.

The author, his wife, and two of his children and their families live in the Nashville, TN area.

WEBSITE: http://www.lifeplanningtools.com

AMAZON: www.amazon.com/author/jswellman

Contact Us

	www.lifeplanningtools.com info@lifeplanningtools.com	Website Email
Facebook	JSWellman	
	www.amazon.com/author/jswellman	**Author Page**
Life Planning Series	www.amazon.com/dp/B09TH9SYC4	
	www.lifeplanningtools.link/newsletter	**Monthly News Letter**

You can help

IDEAS and SUGGESTIONS: If you have a suggestion to improve this book, please let us know.

Mention our LIFE PLANNING books on your social platforms and recommend them to your family and friends.

Thank you!

Make a Difference

The law of prosperity is generosity.
If you want more, give more.
Bob Proctor

Have you ever done something just out of kindness or goodwill without wanting or expecting anything in return? I'm going to ask you to do <u>two things</u> just for that reason. The first will be just out of the goodness of your heart and the second in order to make an impact in someone else's life.

It won't cost you anything and it won't take a lot of time or effort.

This Book
First, what did you think of this book? Give the book an honest review in order for us to compete with the giant publishers. What did you like and how did it impact you? It will only take you several minutes to leave your review at:
https://www.amazon.com/dp/1952359376

Follow the link above to the Amazon sales page, scroll down about three quarters of the page and click the box that says: "Write a customer review." It does not have to be long or well-written – just tell other readers what you think about the book. Or, just score the book on a scale of 1 – 5 stars (5 is high).

This will help us a great deal and we so appreciate your willingness to help. If you want to tell us something about the book directly, you can email us at: info@lifeplanningtools.com.

Give Books to Students and Employees
Secondly, do you know any schools or colleges that might want to give this book to their students or their senior class?

Do you know any companies, churches, or other organizations that would like to give one of our books to their employees or members?

Here is how you can help. If you send us the contact information and allow us to use your name, we will contact the person or persons you suggest with all the details. Obviously there would be special pricing and if the order is large enough, a message from the organization's CEO could be included on the printed pages.

Alternatively, you can personally give a copy of one of our books to the organization for their consideration. We would this book, the Life Planning Handbook, but some organizations might be interested in a specific subject. If they are interested in this partnership with us, they should contact us directly.

It is not that difficult to help someone live a better life: just a little time and intentionality. Let us hear from you if you want to make a difference in someone's life!

J. S. Wellman
Extra-mile Publishing
steve@lifeplanningtools.com
www.lifeplanningtools.com

Made in the USA
Columbia, SC
26 November 2022

72105499R00122